Barbara Wentroble, long recognized for her accuracy in the prophetic, now helps readers learn how to break the enemy's strongholds through prayer. Using sound biblical principles, she shows even the beginner how to pray with a prophetic anointing. A very readable book for both new and seasoned Christians.

QUIN SHERRER

AUTHOR, *HOW TO PRAY FOR YOUR CHILDREN* AND *LISTEN, GOD IS SPEAKING TO YOU*
COLORADO SPRINGS, COLORADO

Prophetic Intercession will stir up your faith, challenge your heart and put action to your prayers. Barbara Wentroble possesses a wealth of experience in the area of the prophetic, and the life-changing stories she shares make her book fun, inspiring and easy to read. Step into the world of the prophetic and be changed!

ALICE SMITH

INTERNATIONAL PRAYER COORDINATOR, U.S. PRAYER TRACK
HOUSTON, TEXAS

Prophetic intercession is an incredibly powerful weapon for waging warfare against an enemy who is blinding the eyes of billions to the glorious light of the gospel. In her powerful book, Barbara Wentroble offers new insights into wielding this mighty weapon to see God's kingdom come and His will done here on earth. If you are wanting to see God's power as never before, read *Prophetic Intercession*!

C. PETER WAGNER

CHANCELLOR, WAGNER LEADERSHIP INSTITUTE
COLORADO SPRINGS, COLORADO

D0172356

Prophetic INTERCESSION

This book is a powerful Kingdom tool for increasing your understanding of prophetic prayer and defeating the powers of darkness. If you need a breakthrough—or know someone who does—read this book.

ELIZABETH ALVES

PRESIDENT, INTERCESSORS INTERNATIONAL
BULVERDE, TEXAS

As an intercessor reading Barbara Wentroble's book *Prophetic Intercession*, I sensed so deeply our created purpose is to know God, to love Him and to do His will. As you read, you will come to know your call more deeply—that you are chosen, appointed and set apart, loved, forgiven and elected by God to be His. This book is a joyous realization of God's gift to intercessors.

BOBBYE BYERLY

DIRECTOR OF PRAYER AND INTERCESSION, WORLD PRAYER CENTER
COLORADO SPRINGS, COLORADO

I've long been convinced one of Scripture's best-kept secrets is the power and potential of prophetic intercession. Barbara Wentroble does a remarkable job of unlocking many of these secrets in her timely and anointed book.

DICK EASTMAN

INTERNATIONAL PRESIDENT, EVERY HOME FOR CHRIST
COLORADO SPRINGS, COLORADO

Prophetic Intercession attests to the power of prayer that is in every believer. Barbara Wentroble's simple but profound teachings equip the reader to unleash the weapon of intercession to overcome any circumstance or foe. In this most strategic time, this book is a "must have" resource guide. I highly recommend *Prophetic Intercession* to the Body of Christ!

KINGSLEY A. FLETCHER

SENIOR PASTOR, LIFE COMMUNITY CHURCH
RESEARCH TRIANGLE PARK, NORTH CAROLINA

God desires for His people to break through enemy barriers and step into a level of authority greater than we have known! Barbara Wentroble shares her own journey in such an inspirational and practical way that you, too, will feel "called higher" to be God's voice in the earth.

JANE HANSEN

PRESIDENT, AGLOW INTERNATIONAL
EDMONDS, WASHINGTON

While many people are *talking* about prophecy and intercession, this biblically based and eye-opening book is a working how-to manual.

CINDY JACOBS

COFOUNDER, GENERALS OF INTERCESSION
COLORADO SPRINGS, COLORADO

Prophetic Intercession is about the type of prayer that manifests the vision and reality of God in the earth's realm, causing entire cities to be transformed, nations to be changed, cancers to subside and families to be made whole. Barbara Wentroble establishes the principles of spiritual breakthrough necessary for any Christian to walk in victory. Read, ask and receive!

CHUCK D. PIERCE

DIRECTOR, WORLD PRAYER CENTER
COLORADO SPRINGS, COLORADO

PROPHETIC INTERCESSION

Prophetic INTERCESSION

Letting God Lead Your Prayers

BARBARA WENTROBLE

Renew

A Division of Gospel Light
Ventura, California, U.S.A.

Published by Regal Books
From Gospel Light
Ventura, California, U.S.A.
Printed in the U.S.A.

Regal Books is a ministry of Gospel Light, an evangelical Christian publisher dedicated to serving the local church. We believe God's vision for Gospel Light is to provide church leaders with biblical, user-friendly materials that will help them evangelize, disciple and minister to children, youth and families.

It is our prayer that this Regal book will help you discover biblical truth for your own life and help you meet the needs of others. May God richly bless you.

For a free catalog of resources from Regal Books/Gospel Light, please call your Christian supplier, or contact us at 1-800-4-GOSPEL, or at www.regalbooks.com.

All Scripture quotations, unless otherwise indicated, are taken from the *New American Standard Bible,* © 1960, 1962, 1963, 1968, 1971, 1972, 1973, 1975, 1977 by The Lockman Foundation. Used by permission.

Other versions used are:
KJV—King James Version. Authorized King James Version.
NIV—Scripture quotations are taken from the *Holy Bible, New International Version®. NIV®.* Copyright © 1973, 1978, 1984 by International Bible Society. Used by permission of Zondervan Publishing House. All rights reserved.
NKJV—Scripture taken from the *New King James Version.* Copyright © 1979, 1980, 1982 by Thomas Nelson, Inc. Publishers. Used by permission. All rights reserved.

Cover Design by Kevin Keller
Interior Design by Robert Williams
Edited by Kathi Mills

LIBRARY OF CONGRESS CATALOGING-IN-PUBLICATION DATA
Wentroble, Barbara, 1943-
    Prophetic intercession / Barbara Wentroble
        p.   cm.
    Includes bibliographical references.
    ISBN 0-8307-2376-5
    1. Intercessory prayer—Christianity.   I. Title.
    BV210.2W44   1999   99-37027
    243—dc21   CIP

6 7 8 9 10 11 12 13 14 15 16 17 18 19 20 / 09 08 07 06 05 04 03

Rights for publishing this book in other languages are contracted by Gospel Light Worldwide, the international nonprofit ministry of Gospel Light. Gospel Light Worldwide also provides publishing and technical assistance to international publishers dedicated to producing Sunday School and Vacation Bible School curricula and books in the languages of the world. For additional information, visit www.gospellightworldwide.org; write to Gospel Light Worldwide, P.O. Box 3875, Ventura, CA 93006; or send an e-mail to info@gospellightworldwide.org.

To my husband and best friend, Dale.

CONTENTS

*Spiritual giants in our lives must be conquered if we are to
see greater breakthroughs in prayer.*

*The river of life flowing from us has the power to break
curses and barrenness afflicting people, cities and territories.*

*Sharp is safe. Dull is dangerous. When the spiritual ax is
sharp, strength is gained for the battle.*

*God reveals prayer needs and gives strategies to overcome
the enemy. Victory will come through obedience to the Lord.*

*Intercessors are God's covenant partners. They are to
speak forgiveness, healing and restoration to the broken
places in the earth.*

*All intercessors are not prophets, but all may receive a
prophetic anointing empowering them to speak the will and
purpose of God into situations.*

FOREWORD

Did you know there are giants in the land? Every day, as Christians, we are faced with enormous opposition—titans, adversaries, Goliaths—that is born in the sinful hearts of humanity and empowered by spiritual powers. Now more than ever, I am convinced that God is asking every believer to be a diligent prayer warrior—a prophetic intercessor—who can shatter the gates of hell and bring God's light of renewal and awakening to a dying world.

There are many ways of praying, and *Prophetic Intercession* captures how believers can listen to the mind and counsel of God. Being able to hear God's voice is a critical component of prayer. Intercession of this nature helps the Body of Christ to act tactically and in crucial moments with great effectiveness against the kingdom of darkness. How many times has the Lord been gracious in letting us know His timing and intent on a person, place and city. How often have we missed His wisdom in events because we weren't listening. Prophetically interceding for a loved one, a stranger, a community or a government is a privilege because we gain front-row seats to God's innermost counsel for humanity.

Prophetic Intercession will take you by the hand and help you to understand the role of prophetic proclamations, acts, music, dancing, shouting, even clapping. There is a connection with all of these prophetic expressions and with intercession. In the same fashion, God spoke to His prophets in the past like

Samuel, Elisha and Daniel. God communicates His will and creatively gives up expression of His will to the Church. This prophetic undercurrent is not something to be feared, but greatly welcomed, because the Lord is sharing the depth of His heart with us.

I can encourage every believer to read this wonderful book! My dear friend Barbara Wentroble has faithfully explored the nature of interceding prophetically. She has pointed out that a person doesn't need to be a prophet to be part of a prophetic anointing in prayer. Prophetic intercession is not confined to a select group; it is for any and all who hunger to act in the midst of His will.

Barbara does not stop there though. She goes the extra mile in emphasizing the importance of such intercession for every ministry! As the gospel spreads to every corner of the world, the Church and various ministerial arms need solid foundations rooted in effective intercession. The lack of prophetic intercession creates a blind side that we cannot afford in church leadership, in one-on-one counseling or in citywide evangelism. We need to have vigilance, diligence and humility as we intercede prophetically for pastors, counselors and evangelists.

Prophetic Intercession offers you a powerful spiritual sling and the stones to slay giants. I invite you to take up this book, read it thoroughly and allow God to deliver the Goliaths into your hand.

PASTOR DUTCH SHEETS

ACKNOWLEDGMENTS

Thank you to those who made it possible for me to write about my incredible journey in prayer:

To my husband, Dale, and my adult children, Brian, Lori and Mark, for being a constant support of love and encouragement. You have made my life a joy beyond measure.

To my father, James Brasell, and in memory of my mother, Lois. You gave me a foundation in life that helped me become who I am today.

To my daughters-in-law, Michelle and Brittanne. You are the ones I prayed for the Lord to send to my two sons. The Lord also sent you to me. To Michelle, who is also my office administrator, for your sensitivity to all my needs and for continuously doing the little extras that make my life and ministry more enjoyable.

To Norma Anderson, who has forfeited sleep and weekends to help me. Your incredible gift for editing gave me the courage to write.

To my prayer coordinator, Brenda Ramsey, for all your prayers, sacrifice and extra efforts to see me accomplish all the Lord has placed in my heart.

To the intercessors who labored in prayer while I wrote.

To all who, for so many years, have encouraged me to write this book.

Finally and above all, to the Lord Jesus Christ, who is my life. Without You I can do nothing!

Chapter One

NEED FOR BREAKTHROUGH

*So David came to Baal-perazim, and defeated them there;
and he said, "The Lord has broken through my enemies before me
like the breakthrough of waters." Therefore he named
that place Baal-perazim.*

2 SAMUEL 5:20

1953. "Breakthrough for Polio." Newspaper headlines throughout the world declared the victory. The enemy that had left untold thousands of people paralyzed, deformed or dead was now conquered.

Dr. Jonas Salk had discovered a vaccine. If taken, the immunization would free future generations from the devastation of this infirmity. The findings of this medical mystery had been costly. Years of research, sleepless nights and hard work had been invested. Now a new epoch of health and wholeness from the dread of polio could begin.

Have you ever read about such breakthroughs in the field of science or medicine and wondered why we do not see similar achievements in our prayer life? To look at longstanding difficulties in the lives of loved ones or in our cities can be discouraging. It can seem to be a hopeless situation when you see that mighty men and women in the past have prayed and the situation they prayed about did not change. Circumstances or valid written reports can leave a sense of defeat. Discouragement can prevent us from praying for an answer. *What if nothing changes? What if I don't pray the right way?*

SEEKING ANSWERS

A feeling of inadequacy gripped my heart as Linda stood in front of me on a Sunday morning at the church altar. A member of our congregation had brought her to church. The faith-filled man had told her, "If you will just come to church, our pastor's wife will pray for you. You will be healed." I was thankful John had confidence in my prayers but overwhelmed at the circumstances in Linda's life. I was even more overwhelmed at my inability to produce the needed miracle.

Linda had been diagnosed with terminal cancer at a hospital in Houston that specialized in the treatment of cancer. She was the mother of small twin girls, and her husband had left her. Linda expressed a fervent desire to live and raise her one-year-old daughters. At the time she was undergoing treatment at the hospital, but the prognosis gave her no hope. "Just get ready to die," she'd been told. "There is nothing else we can do." How those words rang in her ears. Hopelessness seemed to wrap around her like a blanket. She needed a breakthrough. All I knew to do was ask—and ask I did!

Two weeks later Linda returned to the church. In place of the blanket of hopelessness was a covering of light and life. She radiated hope. Running up to me, Linda excitedly gave me the report. After returning to Houston for a week of treatments, she had been given a doctor's report: "Healed." Each time they tested her the doctors declared, "Something is wrong. There is nothing there." This response continued throughout all the tests during that week.

Reminiscing over the prayer time at the church, Linda told me, "I remembered you said, 'Just believe.' I thought, *I tried the doctors. I received chemotherapy. I had x-rays. I did everything I knew to do. I might as well believe.*"

Was it believing that had brought the healing? Was it John's faith in bringing her to church? Was it the anointing with oil and laying on of hands? Was it the spoken word commanding cancer to leave her body? Was it any combination of the above? Sometimes I believe the Lord does things *in spite of us* and not *because of us*. He is God of the impossible who makes all things possible!

When I came into this walk of the fullness of the Holy Spirit, I heard many testimonies and they were always filled with the excitement of immediate answers to prayer.

- "The Lord filled me with His Holy Spirit, and my life changed overnight."
- "I prayed and was healed instantly from cancer."
- "I went to the altar for prayer and was delivered from alcohol and drugs. I have never had a desire for those things since."
- "My pastor prayed for our marriage and the problems just seemed to disappear."

The answers to prayer seemed so simple. It worked for so many others. Why did it not always work for me? Were others' prayers more spiritual than mine? Did those people know a secret I did not know? Why were some answers to prayers immediate and yet it took so long for other prayers to be answered? Through the years I have learned there are times when the Lord brings quick answers to prayer. He performs miracles of healing, deliverance and restoration in a moment of time. Instantaneous answers, however, are not the norm. I have discovered that the Lord is looking for faithful people who are willing to persevere in prayer, to seek Him and His plan for breakthrough.

JODIE'S VISION

I realized I was not the only person who has questioned the Lord concerning the difficulty in breakthrough. Jodie Waggoner was attending a prayer meeting at Rhema Bible School in Tulsa, Oklahoma. The room was filled with people praying. Moving toward the back of the room, she sat down and prayed quietly in the Spirit. The Lord chose that moment to give her a vision, which is much like a dream except that the person is awake when it occurs. The vision, as Jodie relates it, was so clear.

"I first saw a large group of people in prayer, worship and teaching," she explained. "They were doing all they knew to experience God's presence. I felt in my spirit that they were doing the will of the Lord. There was a sense that the people were frustrated, but I could discern their faithfulness. I then realized this was the Body of Christ I was seeing. It was not just the people who were gathered in the room with me.

"The next thing I saw was a huge membrane. It reflected the most beautiful colors of the rainbow. Blue. Green. Purple. All the colors of the rainbow were visible. The colored membrane was fairly translucent, because I could still see everyone underneath.

"As the people prayed and sang, I could see the prayers and songs rise upward into the covering. However, they would only cause the membrane to gently rise up and then it would come back down again. I watched this for a very short time and became concerned that I didn't see what I wanted to see—a breakthrough!

"Soon I seemed to be watching from a great distance and could sense something was about to happen. I cried out, 'God, why are we not breaking through?'

"There was a long moment of silence and the Lord spoke: 'I will bring the breakthrough!' I didn't see His finger but sensed

Him reaching out and touching the membrane. At that moment the membrane split!"

UNDERSTANDING BREAKTHROUGH

What, then, is meant by the word "breakthrough"? *Webster's Dictionary* defines the word this way: "A strikingly important advance or discovery in any field of knowledge or activity; the act, result or place of breaking through against resistance, as in warfare." In the Old Testament David spoke of a time in his life when he experienced a breakthrough from his enemies during a time of warfare. We read about it in 1 Chronicles 14:8-11. The story is also told in 2 Samuel 5:17-20:

> When the Philistines heard that they had anointed David king over Israel, all the Philistines went up to seek out David; and when David heard of it, he went down to the stronghold. Now the Philistines came and spread themselves out in the valley of Rephaim. Then David inquired of the LORD, saying, "Shall I go up against the Philistines? Wilt Thou give them into my hand?" And the LORD said to David, "Go up, for I will certainly give the Philistines into your hand." So David came to Baal-perazim, and defeated them there; and he said, "The LORD has broken through my enemies before me like the breakthrough of waters." Therefore he named that place Baal-perazim.

The word *Baal-perazim* is a word that means master, or lord of the breakthrough. Have you ever needed the Lord to reveal Himself to you as "Lord of the breakthrough"? Have you felt like all the Philistines have been assigned to come against you?

The enemy does not want you to come into your destiny. He wants to stop the vision the Lord has given you. The enemy has heard about the progress in God you are making and he is out to stop it.

The Philistines heard David had been anointed king over Israel. They were stirred up and upset over the news. David's promotion was the fulfillment of a prophetic word given to him as a young lad by the prophet Samuel (see 1 Sam. 16:12,13). He had a destiny to fulfill. Whenever a person, city or nation advances toward its destiny in God, the enemy will seek to hinder. Satan does not want the purposes of God to come to pass.

Abraham also experienced resistance as he came out of Egypt and approached the land of promise:

> And the land could not sustain them while dwelling together; for their possessions were so great that they were not able to remain together. And there was strife between the herdsmen of Abram's livestock and the herdsmen of Lot's livestock. Now the Canaanite and the Perizzite were dwelling then in the land (Gen.13:6,7).

FIGHTING FIVE GIANTS

Warfare is a genuine, necessary part of coming into your destiny. The enemy assigns giants to hinder us from accomplishing God's will for our life. However, David not only encountered giants of resistance, but he also experienced victory.

Second Samuel 5:17 tells us that "*all* the Philistines went up to seek out David." After reading this scripture, I asked the Lord, "Who were the *all* Samuel spoke of?" I discovered through my study that there were five chief cities among the Philistines: Ashdod, Gaza, Ashkelon, Gath and Ekron (see 1 Sam. 6:17-18).

The number five represents grace. The Lord is going to give grace to His Church to defeat every giant opposing His people! Before we can be as effective as we need to be in intercession, these giants must be overcome. These five Philistine cities, representing the five giants or enemies that David faced and defeated, were pride, self-rule, greed or selfishness, distractions and the winepress.

ASHDOD

The first giant David destroyed was Ashdod. The ark of God was carried to Ashdod after their victory at Ebenezer. It was then taken to the temple of Dagon (see 1 Sam. 5:1,2). The word Ashdod means "city on a hill." It represents a high and lofty place. The enemy called "pride" will seek to prevent a person or nation from reaching its destiny. Proverbs 16:18 says, "Pride goes before destruction, And a haughty spirit before stumbling."

Citizens of Argentina can remember the days of Pride before the invasion of the Falkland Islands in 1982. God used this defeat of Argentina to break the back of pride in that nation. Since that time, the country has been in a state of continual revival. The Church has had a breakthrough.

A spirit of meekness and humility will position us for a breakthrough. Jesus taught the principle of functioning in an opposite spirit from the enemy to enjoy victory:

> And if Satan casts out Satan, he is divided against himself; how then shall his kingdom stand? (Matt. 12:26).

Humility is the opposite of pride. The spirit of humility will defeat the enemy called "pride."

GAZA

The second giant seeking to prevent breakthrough is one named Gaza. Gaza was the capital city of the Philistines. This giant represents government. The question is always, Who is in charge? Self always wants to sit on the throne. It seeks to have its own way. Nevertheless, self-rule must give way to His rulership if we are to defeat the enemy.

Have you ever noticed that most of the time we like to make our own decisions? Human nature just doesn't like other people telling it what to do. This independent spirit was evident at the time of the Judges when "everyone did what was right in his own eyes" (Judg. 21:25).

The philosophy of self-rule is even taught to our children in many school systems today. It is called "situational ethics." A younger generation is being taught to make decisions based on their own individual sense of judgment. According to this philosophy, a person becomes the authority who decides what is right and what is wrong. In the life of a Christian, it is not always a sin issue that the Lord is dealing with. He wants us to choose the best and not settle for the good. To do that, Jesus must be acknowledged as King and Supreme Ruler in every decision. A good soldier must be willing to be obedient to the commander in the midst of warfare. If he continues to make his own independent choices, he can be wounded or defeated in the war.

ASHKELON

Another giant David had to face was Ashkelon. This giant represents prosperity or fertility. It also speaks of greed and selfishness, which breeds fear of losing material possessions or even relationships. That fear can keep us from giving ourselves totally to God's purposes. It will try to get us to hold back from serious warfare praying.

- *What will happen to my family if I engage in spiritual warfare?*
- *I heard of someone who got involved in spiritual warfare and they went bankrupt. Could this happen to me?*

- *I am so busy. I don't know if I really can spend the time necessary to pray for a breakthrough. If God is as powerful as the Bible
says He is, can't He just do what he wants to do without me?*

Part of the enemy's defeat arises from an understanding of
our position in covenant with God. All we have is God's, and all
He has is ours. There is no reason to fear, if we understand His
provision and protection. Walking in a revelation of covenant
relationship with the Lord releases a spirit of liberality. Giving of
finances, time, ability and material possessions is a way of life in
the kingdom of God.

I remember the 1969 Karman Ghia car we once owned. After
driving it for about ten years, my husband repaired it and gave it
to a couple who needed a car. They drove it on the mission field
for about five more years. After that, it was repaired and given to
their son. The last time we heard about the car, it was still being
driven after about 20 years of service. As we are willing to give the
way the early Church did in the book of Acts, the Lord will supply
every need. A spirit of greed and selfishness hinders God from
breaking through.

Sometimes the most important area of giving is the one
where we give time in intercession. The very word *intercession*
means we are praying for someone else. Intercession is the most
selfless thing we can do. It breaks the back of the giant of *selfishness*.

GATH

A fourth giant to be overcome is Gath. It is a word that means
"winepress." The difficulties that we are experiencing are being
used by the Lord to prepare us for the new wine. In biblical times
grapes were put into the winepress and then walked on to release
the wine. Do you ever feel you have been walked on? Does the
pressure from life cause you to think everything in you has been

poured out? Could it be that the Lord is taking these difficulties and turning them into new wine to bring refreshment and restoration to others?

We have not tasted all of the "new" that the Lord has reserved for this generation. I sometimes look at the wonderful things the Lord has done in my life. When Jesus healed our two-year-old baby boy, it was a miracle. The doctors recorded the healing in medical records. When Jesus filled me with His precious Spirit, it was as if I had just started to live. Yet with all that He did for my family and me in the past, He has saved the best until now.

> And when the headwaiter tasted the water which had become wine, and did not know where it came from (but the servants who had drawn the water knew), the head-waiter called the bridegroom, and said to him, "Every man serves the good wine first, and when men have drunk freely, then that which is poorer; you have kept the good wine until now" (John 2:9,10).

Ask the Lord to take every hard, difficult place in your life and cause it to become a winepress for the new wine. Jesus was willing to lay down His life so that He might become the Intercessor. He is now asking us to do the same. Do not allow Gath to rob you of the best the Lord has for you.

When the Philistines came against David, he asked the Lord if He would give them into his hands. The Lord answered David by saying He would surely give the Philistines into his hands. David heard the Lord. He had his answer. Because he heard the word of the Lord and was obedient, he experienced break-through. The key to experiencing breakthrough is hearing and obeying the voice of the Lord. Sometimes this type of praying is called *prophetic intercession*.

EKRON

A fifth giant hindering breakthrough is one named Ekron. The name means "extermination." The fly-god was worshiped in Ekron (see 2 Kings 1:2—Baal-Zebub means "Lord of the flies"). Have you ever noticed what happens when a small fly gets into a room? I remember being in a meeting and listening to a dynamic speaker. He was at the most important part of the message. Suddenly, a small fly began to buzz around his face. The audience, who a few seconds before had been captivated by his words, now became completely distracted. Their attention was on that fly—everyone wanted to see if it would land on the speaker's face. How did the fly get into the room? Would anyone be able to remove it? As their attention turned to the fly, the audience missed the most important part of the message. Our focus must be on obtaining a breakthrough and not allowing distractions to keep us from the assignment the Lord has given us.

PROPHETIC INTERCESSION

I remember when I first started praying prophetically. There were no books on prophetic intercession that I knew about. In fact, I didn't know I prayed any differently from others until one day while attending a conference. The speaker I was praying for turned to me and asked, "Did you know that you are praying prophetically?" It was the first time I realized there are many ways to pray. Prophetic intercession is one type of prayer that unlocks miracles and releases the blessings of God. It may be new to many people, but as we search throughout the Bible we can find many examples.

The Body of Christ stands today in the womb of the dawn of a new day (see Ps. 110:3). We are birthing prayers that have the power to break through. When a new mother gives birth to a child, she does not have to be an expert. She simply does what a doctor or midwife instructs her to do and she gets results.

I have spent a great deal of time over the past several years

> WHEN A NEW MOTHER GIVES BIRTH, SHE DOES NOT HAVE TO BE AN EXPERT ON CHILDBIRTH TO GET RESULTS. TODAY THE HOLY SPIRIT IS LEADING AN INEXPERIENCED BODY OF CHRIST TO BIRTH PRAYERS THAT HAVE THE POWER TO BREAK THROUGH.

just doing what I thought the Great Physician said, and that was to "ask." Maybe you have done the same thing. Dr. Jonas Salk, the discoverer of the polio vaccine, dedicated his life to finding a breakthrough. I am sure he asked many questions before he came up with the right answers. He probably made some mistakes along the way. However, he kept on asking. He kept on looking. Finally, the door of breakthrough opened. Jesus told us to do the same thing:

> And I say to you, ask, and it shall be given to you; seek, and you shall find; knock, and it shall be opened to you (Luke 11:9).

Today is a time when knowledge is increasing in the earth (see Dan. 12:4). Before most computer products are available in the stores, they are already obsolete. Engineers continually discover new ways to cause electronic products to do a better job in a shorter time. How we need the Lord to bring revelation to the

Church in order for breakthroughs to happen as a result of our intercession!

In response to Jesus' request for us to ask, let us pray for the Spirit of God to teach us how to experience a breakthrough with our prayers. Let the Holy Spirit teach us to pray prophetically.

Father, we come to you in the name that is above all other names. It is the name above sickness and disease, the name above all forms of bondage, the name above all torment, the name above all unrighteousness. In the powerful name that brought a breakthrough 2,000 years ago, we are asking for the same power to be released today.

We confess we don't know how to pray the way we should. However, we have the promise from Your Word. Romans 8:26,27 says, "And in the same way the Spirit also helps our weakness; for we do not know how to pray as we should, but the Spirit Himself intercedes for us with groanings too deep for words; and He who searches the hearts knows what the mind of the Spirit is, because He intercedes for the saints according to the will of God."

We confess, Lord, that we don't know how to pray. We have tried to pray the way others have prayed. We have read a lot of books. We have attended a lot of seminars. We have fasted. We have done a lot of religious things. Now we stand in need of you. Speak to us. Counsel us, Mighty Counselor.

Our hearts are burdened for people who need the Lord. Our cities are in ruin. Nations are in turmoil. Nevertheless, we know You have the answer. Show us how to get Your answer to those in need. Show us how to rebuild our cities. Show us how to release Your glory to the nations. What we are really asking is, please bring revelation on how to break through the impossible with the power of answered prayer.

We ask You to do it in our generation, Lord. We don't want You to wait and raise up another generation to do what You have asked us to do. Give us not just more information, but give us revelation. In response to these answered prayers may Your name be exalted in the earth! In Jesus' name we pray, Amen!

QUESTIONS FOR CONSIDERATION:

1. What are some areas in your life where the giant Ashdod operates? Is there a root of pride that needs to be cut? Describe a situation where this giant hindered God's purposes in your life.

2. Is there a giant of Gaza who seeks to prevent you from reaching your destiny? What are some areas where you tend to lean on your own strength and understanding rather than seeking the counsel of the Lord?

3. Does the giant called Ashkelon have a place in your life? Ask the Lord to reveal any place where greed or selfishness dominates. Have you truly given your life and your possessions as a sacrifice to the Lord, or do you still hold on to your own desires?

4. What are some of the distractions that hinder you from being effective in prayer? Does the giant Ekron rule, or have you learned how to slay him? What have you done to prevent these distractions from gaining your attention?

5. Have you discerned the work of the Spirit in the midst of difficulties? Has the giant Gath caused you to become bitter or better? Give several examples of how the Lord has used the winepress to make you better.

Chapter Two

THE RIVER OF GOD
BREAKS CURSES

He who believes in Me, as the Scripture said, "From his innermost being shall flow rivers of living water."

JOHN 7:38

"Behold, My river!" The words rang in my ears as if it had been an audible voice. Yet I knew that no one else on the airplane heard it but me. Somehow, I knew it was the voice of God.

It was September 1979. I was fairly new in this "spirit-filled" walk and very new in ministry. Hearing the voice of the Lord had become an exciting adventure. After being raised in a church that told me God doesn't talk today, each experience in hearing His voice proved to me how very near and personal the Lord is to His people. Now He was saying something to me that I did not fully understand. But, behold His river I would attempt to do!

I was on my way to speak in a meeting in New Orleans. Looking out the window of the plane, I saw the mighty Mississippi River below. The Lord revealed much about rivers to me on that late afternoon flight. He said something I would never forget, even though at the time I did not understand the meaning: "In the next move of My Spirit it will be important to keep your eye on the river. Never think you know all about the moving of My Spirit. If you do, and you turn your eye from My river, the river may change direction and you will be on dry ground."

This directive from the Lord concerned me for two reasons. The first reason was that I did not know the Lord had different moves of His Spirit. I was not aware that there are times and seasons on God's calendar. These are strategic times when God wants to do something in the earth. The sons of Issachar understood this principle:

> And of the sons of Issachar, men who understood the times, with knowledge of what Israel should do (1 Chron. 12:32).

THE RIGHT PRAYER FOR THE RIGHT SEASON

The Lord's instruction to me was to receive an Issachar anointing so I would know what the Church was to do and how to pray in critical times. The way to pray in one season is not the way to pray in another season. Farmers know they must do different things in each season. One season is designed for planting, while another season is made for harvesting. It is important to do the right thing in the proper season. Equally important is how we pray in each season.

Dutch Sheets identifies these strategic times and seasons in his book *Intercessory Prayer*:

> This facet of intercession is not only to be something we do on a general regular basis for our family and loved ones. There are also specific times when the Holy Spirit will alert us to particular situations that need protective prayer. These are what the scriptures call *kairos* times.
>
> There are two Greek words for "time." One is *chronos*, which is time in general; the general "time in

which anything is done." The other word, *kairos*, is the strategic or right time; the opportune point of time at which something should be done.

A window of opportunity would be *kairos* time.

A well-timed attack in war would be *kairos* time.

When someone is in danger or about to be attacked by Satan, that is a *kairos* time.

What time it is would be *chronos* time.[1]

I remember a time when my mother-in-law experienced a flow of the river of intercession during a very strategic moment. She was sitting in her living room at 9:30 A.M. Suddenly, she felt a sensation of fear and danger, accompanied by an urgency to pray for her son (my husband) Dale. At first she did not understand where this was coming from. Recognizing she had nothing to fear and was not in danger, she asked the Lord to reveal what this was. This was a wise and necessary move, because gaining understanding is an important first step in effective prayer. An inner prompting will alert you to something your mind does not quite comprehend. At these times just ask the Lord to help you know how He wants you to pray.

After asking the Lord to reveal to her how to pray, Dale's mom then felt a deep impression that it was Dale who was in danger. She prayed for several minutes and then felt the "burden" lift. Later that night she called our home to ask Dale what he had been doing at 9:30 in the morning. "Oh, that's easy," he replied. "I remember because I looked at my watch. Another man was talking to me while we were standing out in the plant at work. There had been some remodeling in the plant over the past several weeks, and we were discussing the progress. All of a sudden I felt an urgency to move from the place where we were standing. We quickly moved to another spot about 20 feet away.

Just as quickly as we moved, a large steel beam fell from the ceiling and landed in the very spot where I had been standing."

A strategic moment! Often I have wondered what would have happened if Dale's mom had not sought the Lord and received her instructions for prayer. Would Dale and the other man be alive? Could they have been paralyzed or deformed from the injury? How many tragedies occur each day because we do not know how to hear the Lord speak so that we can respond in prayer?

FLOWING IN GOD'S CURRENT

The next reason for concern on the plane that day was that I wanted to be sure I was not on dry ground when the river of God was flowing in other places. I wanted to be part of this glorious release in the earth. My prayer that day was, "Lord, make me sensitive to the leading of Your Spirit. Deliver me from any religious spirits that can block me from being part of what You are doing." The Lord has been faithful through these last few years to continue to instruct me about His river. I still do not have all the answers, but I am grateful for His leading.

> There is a river whose streams make glad the city of God,
> the holy dwelling places of the Most High. God is in the
> midst of her, she will not be moved; God will help her
> when morning dawns (Ps. 46:4,5).

As a spiritual type of the city of God, or Zion, the Lord has released a river in us, His Church. According to Deuteronomy 29:22-28, dry ground was the result of a curse that came from not obeying God. A curse was the opposite of the blessings promised by God to those who walked according to His Word. Dry, desert ground produces barrenness and unfruitfulness. Spiritually, not flowing with the river of God produces that same dry ground and barrenness in us today. But the Lord has made a way for the curse of barrenness or unfruitfulness to be broken. He has formed a river in His people to flow out from them to bring fruitfulness to the barren places of the earth.

> He who believes in Me, as the Scripture said, "From his innermost being shall flow rivers of living water" (John 7:38).

This river is an instrument in breaking the curse of dry ground. As we hear the Word of the Lord and then let it flow from us in intercession and prophetic proclamations, fruitfulness will replace the barrenness.

The word "midst" in Psalm 46 is the Hebrew word *qereb*. The *Hebrew-Greek Key Study Bible* refers to this word in the "Lexical Aids to the Old Testament":

> It means the nearest part, the center. . . . *Qereb* is predominant in the Pentateuch, especially in Deuteronomy, but it also appears in Psalms. In Genesis 18:12 it is the inward part of the body which is the seat of laughter.[2]

IRRIGATING THE BARRENNESS

In her time and culture, Sarah, the wife of Abraham, was a woman who was considered cursed because of her barrenness. When the Word of the Lord, the river of God, touched her midst, she laughed. Why was she laughing? Because the curse had been broken! The river broke the curse of barrenness and released the blessing of fruitfulness. Breakthrough made Sarah glad.

How we need the release of fruitfulness in our homes, in our cities and in our nation! If we examine the historical record, it is absolutely clear that the Pilgrims believed that God had led them to this land to pioneer a country with a foundation of a biblical moral order:

> America cannot be rightly understood without first understanding that the early settlers established what can be best described as a "Christian Commonwealth." John Winthrop appealed to God's "Commandments, Ordinances, and Laws" as the philosophical and moral foundation of this early social experiment. Such a society was to be biblically centered. Of this there is no question. No other choice was possible: "Therefore, let us choose life," Winthrop declared, "that we, and our Seed, may live; by obeying his voice, and cleaving to him for he is our life and prosperity" (Deut. 30:19,20).
>
> The ethical system adopted by Americans and embedded in their social order rested on the bedrock of a biblical moral order. This is the essence of the Christian America claim. To say it another way, the Bible served as the ethical foundation for the young Republic, even for those who did not profess the Christian religion.[3]

How sad when we look back to the vision of our forefathers and then see the conditions in our homes and cities today. We should not be surprised, since the Lord showed us in His Word the results of a nation abandoning God:

> Now the generation to come, your sons who rise up after you and the foreigner who comes from a distant land, when they see the plagues of the land and the diseases

with which the Lord has afflicted it, will say, "All its land is brimstone and salt, a burning waste, unsown and unproductive, and no grass grows in it, like the overthrow of Sodom and Gomorrah, Admah and Zeboiim, which the Lord overthrew in His anger and in His wrath." And all the nations shall say, "Why has the LORD done thus to this land? Why this great outburst of anger?" Then men shall say, "Because they forsook the covenant of the Lord, the God of their fathers, which He made with them when He brought them out of the land of Egypt. And they went and served other gods and worshiped them, gods whom they have not known and whom He had not allotted to them. Therefore, the anger of the Lord burned against that land, to bring upon it every curse which is written in this book; and the Lord uprooted them from their land in anger and in fury and in great wrath, and cast them into another land, as it is this day" (Deut. 29:22-28).

Cutting off water is considered a judgment, or curse. The prophet Elijah stood before King Ahab and pronounced judgment by drought. Judgments, however, can be reversed by repentance. Nineveh, when warned by Jonah of God's impending judgment, repented, and the judgment due them was averted. The Lord always warns us of impending judgment so that we can repent, turn and be restored. His desire is for the people to enjoy His blessings and not live under a curse. Over the past number of years I believe there has been a spirit of repentance in our nation. Out of the hearts and mouths of God's people a river of repentance has been released. In the same way that the river flowed from the Garden of Eden to heal and restore the whole earth, the river from the mouths of believers can turn any evil situation around and loose restoration.

A River of Fire

I remember a prophecy told to me in 1994 by Chuck Pierce. He had just returned from speaking at a meeting in Houston. While ministering, the Lord gave him a vision and spoke a prophetic word through him. The word from the Lord said that the next 24 days would be critical. God was looking at Houston and would break structures that were holding back revelation. He said the revelation would be released like rain.

The prophecy continued to say that as the people looked, a river would begin to rise in the east. A literal fire would be on the river and come to the city. There was instruction for intercessors to gather together and pray during the night. The prayers would limit the destruction that would come to the area.

God was calling intercessors to pray for 24 days. Deborah DeGar, an intercessor from the Houston area, alerted local churches. She also led a prayer meeting from 3:00 A.M. to 6:00 A.M. during those 24 days.

Exactly 24 days later, Houston experienced one of the worst floods recorded in the history of the city. The San Jacinto River, east of the city, flooded throughout Houston. A gas line broke and caused a literal fire on the river. As a result of the prophetic warning followed by the fulfillment of the prophetic word, the city experienced a new move of the Holy Spirit.

Do we always see a *literal* river? No. Is the manifestation of restoration always immediate? No. Does this river flowing from the innermost part of God's people in prayer always accomplish its purpose? Yes. Solomon described the Bride Church like a river:

You are a garden spring, A well of fresh water, And streams flowing from Lebanon (Song of Sol. 4:15).

A RIVER OF HEALING

I remember seeing this river bringing healing to a man for whom the doctors had no hope. John came on a Sunday night to the church where my husband and I pastored. He walked slowly, using a cane for support. John shared his frustration about his current medical situation. Not only did he have extreme difficulty in walking, but hardly any organ in his body worked properly. He was plagued with diabetes, high blood pressure, kidney problems, heart problems and many other maladies. His hospital records showed that he spent two to three weeks out of each month in the hospital. The doctors offered no solution and had resigned themselves to simply maintaining him as long as possible. For John, this did not sound like life; it sounded like living death.

THE RIVER OF GOD FLOWING
FROM THE INNERMOST PART OF HIS
PEOPLE IN PRAYER WILL ALWAYS
ACCOMPLISH ITS PURPOSE.

Since we had prayer at the church each morning at 6:00, we invited him to come. John became our "river project." If God's power worked the way the Bible says it does, it should work for John.

Each morning, following the prayer time at church, the entire group would lay hands on John and pray for a release of God's river to flow from us and into his sick body. We truly believed that the Lord could turn this unfruitful body into one that was healed and restored. Was that too hard for the God who made his body in the beginning? We didn't think so!

Gradually, over a period of several months, we saw the miracle of restoration. The first thing to go was the cane. Strength replaced weakness. Next, the chemistry of his body started changing. Hospital visits were less frequent. Within a year, John changed from a hopeless, infirm individual with no hope for a future to one with energy to spare. He was at the church each time the doors were opened. What joy to see him involved with so many activities and devoting his time and energy to the Lord's purposes. The "river project" proved successful.

POSTPONED ANSWERS

Why do we not always get the same positive results? Is it because God has favorite people? Why don't all people get healed? I once heard that Kathryn Kuhlman said this would be the first question she would ask when she got to heaven.

We may not have all the answers to our questions, but there are some principles in the Bible that help us in our journey to break curses and release a river of restoration in the earth. Dutch Sheets has some helpful insights toward reaching a breakthrough:

> Certain amounts of this power or river of life must be released in the realm of the spirit to accomplish certain things. Different amounts are required for different things. Just as in the natural you need different levels of power for different things, so it is in the spirit realm. It is like the difference between the amount of power it takes to light a flashlight versus a building, or a building as opposed to a city. The same is true in the spirit. Different amounts of God's power are needed to accomplish certain things. [4]

As intercessors release the river from their innermost being through prophetic prayer, proclamations and various other prophetic means, the earth is going to experience the breaking of curses from people, cities and nations. The breaking of curses will result in the flow of restoration and blessings. Harvest will come in, and the earth will be filled with God's glory.

THE RIVER RELEASED

I remember a time when Dale and I attended a meeting in another town with several friends. As we were driving home late at night, we decided to find a place to stop for coffee. Who wants to go home after such a glorious evening in the presence of the Lord? We just wanted to linger in the afterglow of the evening.

Stopping at the only place open in this small town, we entered the Mineola Cafe. It looked just like its name—small, old, worn and filled with cigarette smoke, while the sound of country music filled the atmosphere.

As we sat down, I noticed a table close by where about a half-dozen people were sitting. My eyes were drawn to one of the women. She sat there wearing clothing that looked as if it came from the garbage heap. Looking her way, I heard the Lord speak to me. It was not an audible voice; however, there were very distinct words inside me: "I want you to minister to her." Being new in this walk of the fullness of the spirit, I didn't know what it meant to "minister." *What was I supposed to do? What if I did it wrong?*

After a few moments of silently letting the Lord know I didn't know how to minister to her, I started bargaining with God. Have you ever tried to get God to change His mind? If so, you know I didn't get very far. Finally, I thought I had a deal so difficult God couldn't possibly do anything about it. *If You will cause that lady to get up and come over to my table, I will minister to her.* There! I knew this was too hard even for God. Wrong! Just as I finished my statement, the lady got out of her chair and walked straight over to me. "I need to put these quarters in the jukebox," she informed me. God had done what I thought was impossible.

"After you put your quarters in the jukebox, please come back and let me talk to you," I responded. Within a few minutes she was back. I invited her to go with me to a nearby table so we could be alone. The whole time I quietly prayed for the Lord to show me how to be obedient to Him. God is looking for people who will just trust Him each step of the way. As we are obedient to take the first step, He will reveal the next step.

"Tell her I love her," the Lord instructed.

"The Lord sent me here tonight to tell you He loves you," I said.

"No," she replied. "He couldn't possibly love me."

Thinking my assignment was over, I let the Lord know I had told her what He said and that she didn't believe it.

"Tell her again that I love her," the Lord instructed. Once more I repeated the words I had heard on the inside. Once more she refused to accept what was spoken. Then He added more information. "Tell her she used to know Me. She used to walk with Me."

After I spoke the words of the Lord to the lady, tears started streaming down her face. "You're right. I did know the Lord. I walked with Him; I loved Him. But, you don't know what happened to me. My husband left me. I had small children to raise. I had no way of making money. I became a prostitute to get money to feed my children. God couldn't possibly love me."

After sharing with this barren, dry, fruitless woman the forgiveness of the Lord as recorded in 1 John 1:9, I prayed with her. She confessed her sin of trusting in herself for her needs rather than trusting in the Lord. She repented and made a fresh commitment to the Lord. I then sensed something more. "I see the Lord bringing healing in your body," I said.

"It's my heart! It's my heart! I feel it. The Lord is healing my heart," she exclaimed, as she slumped over under the power of the Holy Spirit in the booth at the Mineola Cafe.

What happened? The river of God was released. Harvest had come in. A woman living under the curse of poverty, shame and reproach had been forgiven and had allowed God to come in and begin the process of healing and restoration. In place of barrenness, God began to bring blessings and abundant life.

What works for an individual will work for a city or a nation. The Lord is showing us how to release His river to break curses and bring restoration. May that river flow from the Church into all the earth!

Father, I ask You to release Your river in me. I don't have all the answers about how it works, I just know You said it would. Let me be an instrument of healing and restoration in the earth. Deliver me from fears, inadequacies and complacency. Help me to venture into the unknown in prayer. What is unknown to me is known to You. You have all knowledge. You are all wisdom. Let Your river flow through me. Break curses and bring healing and restoration for Your glory!

QUESTIONS FOR CONSIDERATION:

1. What do you believe was the purpose of the river in the Garden of Eden? How was this river to affect desert places? What are some desert places you see in the lives of people? in cities? in nations?

2. Do you think the Lord brings judgment today? Why? If God is a God of love, why does He allow disasters and calamities to come to people?

3. What is a curse? According to Scripture, why do curses

occur? Do you see evidence of a curse in our nation? in other nations?

4. Describe the river in God's people. Have you ever experienced it? What were the results?

5. How do you think this river is involved in harvest? Is it necessary? Why can't we just preach and bring in the harvest? How did Jesus and the Early Church reach the harvest?

Chapter Three

STRENGTH TO BREAK THROUGH

For Thou hast girded me with strength for battle; Thou hast subdued under me those who rose up against me.

2 SAMUEL 22:40

"Sharp is safe. Dull is dangerous." I stood at the deli counter in my local supermarket looking at the sign. It was placed in a very visible spot, just above the meat slicer. While the butcher sliced the smoked turkey and cheese, I pondered the meaning of the sign. Knives that were sharp seemed more dangerous to me than dull ones. But the more I thought about it, the more I realized I needed to change my mind. To be sharp is to be safe; to be dull is dangerous.

SHARP IS SAFE

This is what God's Word says about sharpness:

> If the axe is dull and he does not sharpen its edge, then he must exert more strength. Wisdom has the advantage of giving success (Eccles. 10:10).

Much time and energy can be wasted trying to pray for situations when our spiritual ax is dull.

Webster defines "dull" as "lacking sensitivity; blunted in

feeling or perception." Webster also gives this synonym of the word: "Dull is specifically applied to a point or edge that has lost its previous sharpness (a *dull* knife) and generally connotes a lack of keenness, zest, spirit, intensity, etc."[1]

A gardener does not wait until he is in the process of mowing before he sharpens his blade. Before he begins his task, the blade needs to be sharp; otherwise, he will be required to exert more energy and time to get the job done. Likewise, intercessors should keep sharp. A mind that has not been renewed or a spirit that has lost its sensitivity can keep a person from sharp perception during prayer.

I once read the story of someone who approached a man who was cutting down a tree. He had been working at the task for five hours and was tired from all the hard work. When asked why he did not stop and sharpen his saw, he replied that he did not have time; he was too busy sawing. Many times we are the same way; we are working hard at the task. But if we took the time to increase our sharpness, we could get the job done in less time with less effort.

Sharpening our spiritual saw involves a spiritual sensitivity so we will have eyes to see, ears to hear and a heart to understand what the Spirit is saying to us. Spiritual sensitivity is a vital part of effective intercession.

Jesus talked about hearing ears and seeing eyes when teaching His disciples about the kingdom of heaven:

And in their case the prophecy of Isaiah is being fulfilled, which says, "You will keep on hearing, but will not understand; and you will keep on seeing, but will not perceive; for the heart of this people has become dull, and with their ears they scarcely hear, and they have closed their eyes lest they should see with their eyes, and hear with their ears, and understand with their heart and return, and I should heal them." But blessed are your eyes, because they see; and your ears, because they hear. For truly I say to you, that many prophets and righteous men desired to see what you see, and did not see it; and to hear what you hear, and did not hear it (Matt. 13:14-17).

SPIRITUAL FINE-TUNING

Today the Lord is revealing to us many things that the prophets of old wanted to see. Isaiah saw a people who refused to hear and see what God wanted to reveal to them. Because of refusal to hear, their hearts became callused, their ears became dull of hearing and their eyes were blinded. Religious people of Jesus' day displayed the same malady. Yet He speaks of a people who are able to see, hear and understand what the Lord is saying to them. These people are sharp like a freshly sharpened ax or knife. Intercessors need to be in this category of sharpness.

Years ago we played a game where a circle of people was formed. The first person would whisper a sentence to the one seated on the left. That person then repeated what he heard in the ear of the one on his left. The procedure continued until the last person listened to the words whispered in his ear. He then would tell the group what he heard. A roar of laughter would go up from the circle. Each person had heard something a little different from what each of the others had heard. It was always amazing how different the statement was from the first person who heard it until the last person who heard it! The ears just could not hear exactly what was being said. Is it possible a similar thing happens with spiritual hearing?

Sharpness in spiritual hearing requires practice and perseverance. I sometimes refer to developing a sharp spirit as "fine-tuning." Do you remember the early days of radio and TV, before the modern digital technology of today? Radios sometimes emitted a sound called "static." Whenever anyone turned on the radio and it was not quite tuned to the right frequency, it made an awful noise. "Turn it down!" everyone yelled. The music or words spoken were irritating to the listener. Why? The radio was not fine-tuned to the right frequency.

The Lord has made a way for His people to fine-tune their spirits to the Lord. The writer of the book of Hebrews refers to this when warning against the danger of spiritual laziness:

> Concerning him we have much to say, and it is hard to explain, since you have become dull of hearing. For though by this time you ought to be teachers, you have need again for someone to teach you the elementary principles of the oracles of God, and you have come to need milk and not solid food. For everyone who partakes only of milk is not accustomed to the word of righteousness, for he is a babe. But solid food is for the mature, who because of practice have their senses trained to discern good and evil (Heb. 5:11-14).

How then do we practice and have our spiritual senses trained?

· Do we go to a spiritual "gym"?
· What spiritual "muscles" have to be built up?
· Is "stretching" part of the training?
· What are some of the things that can keep my spiritual senses dull?
· Do I need "workout clothes" for this exercise?

SHARPENED BY WISDOM

Wisdom directs on how to sharpen our ax and put an edge on us to cut through obstacles that hinder breakthrough in intercession. The wisdom of the Lord will bring victory and peace. Someone once said, "In the time of wisdom there is peace, but from the lack of knowledge and understanding war will come."

A CLEANSED HEART

How then do I gain wisdom and sharpen my spiritual senses? The first way is to allow a cleansing of my heart and life. Cleansing is a lifelong process. Although we are cleansed from the sin of rejecting Jesus at the moment of the new birth, there must be a daily cleansing of the dirt we pick up on life's journey. This is where we many times resist the prompting of the Lord—especially if we feel justified in our unforgiveness, resentments, offenses, etc. We sometimes want to hold onto these attitudes rather than allow the Holy Spirit to convict and bring cleansing to our life.

Dale's mother told me a story about trying to get him to take a bath when he was still a young boy. Each day at bath time he tried to talk her out of it. "I had a bath yesterday," he reminded her. Yet she wouldn't give up her insistence on daily baths. "As long as you live in this house, you will have a bath each day," she exhorted. Guess who won? Mother, of course. Guess who is going to win when we insist that we have already been cleansed? The Lord, through the power of the Holy Spirit, of course! Because of His stubborn love, He will not give up on us.

In the book of Joshua the Lord did not let the tribe of Israel get away with things He told them not to do. In Joshua 7 the whole nation of Israel was hindered in war because of sin in the camp. This situation was the first instance of disobedience in the

Promised Land. Although one man committed the offense, all Israel was involved and felt the consequences of sin. Israel's defeat at Ai was not a failure of God's promises; it was caused by one man's disobedience. This is a concept that is hard for us, in our "American individualism," to understand. But God's Word is quite clear that, although there is individual responsibility for sin, there is also a corporate responsibility and a corporate consequence.

Cleansing had to take place before the enemies could be defeated. The Lord said to Joshua:

> Rise up! Consecrate the people and say, "Consecrate yourselves for tomorrow, for thus the LORD, the God of Israel, has said, 'There are things under the ban in your midst, O Israel. You cannot stand before your enemies until you have removed the things under the ban from your midst'" (Josh. 7:13).

There are times when we need an individual cleansing, and there are times when we need a corporate cleansing before victory can be achieved.

DELIVERANCE FROM FEAR

The next area where we can sharpen our senses involves deliverance (being set free) from fear. Fear will seek to paralyze us as we advance toward the enemy. Fear will keep us from using the spiritual weapons available to us as believers. Arthur Matthews quotes Robert Jackson when he says, "On the battlefield the real enemy is fear and not the bayonet and the bullet."[2]

A friend of mine was ministering in a church two years after the death of the pastor's wife. From outward appearances it looked as if the church had experienced healing and restoration. Praise and worship had reached a new level. The congregation had reached a place of knowing they were ready for a new break-through. Excitement filled the air! However, my friend Barbara Yoder sensed something was holding them back from the break-through.

After praying over the situation, she felt the Lord gave her insight. Now she needed the wisdom of the Lord to confront the predicament. What if she were wrong? What if the people were not ready to deal with the matter and things got worse? These are questions that will keep us from handling confrontation with the enemy. Barbara had to step out in faith, knowing that the Lord had revealed the tactic of the enemy and given her the strategy for breakthrough in the church.

Barbara spoke to the church that evening and told them what she had sensed in her spirit. The church had reached a place of breakthrough several times in the past. They were at the point of a major breakthrough when the pastor's wife died. She was young and greatly loved by the congregation, but then she was gone. Now they were at another point of breakthrough. What if once again something painful happened? Was it worth the price? Hidden fear lurked behind the smiling, joyful faces. Only the Spirit of the Lord could reveal the concealed enemy.

The people had been going through the right motions and yet had halted at a place just before breakthrough. After Barbara addressed the situation, a revelation came that a "blanket" of grief was on them, which they did not realize. The grief was hold-ing their spirits in captivity. A wave of release came on the peo-ple as they fell on their faces. They confessed their fears of mov-ing to another level of success. The Lord poured out His healing love and brought restoration. Since that time, the church has experienced one victory after another. The Lord has even given the pastor a new wife who is loved and admired by the entire congregation.

The Lord has made a way for us to be delivered from fear. As we meditate on His Word and resist the lies of the enemy, we experience freedom from fear. Our trust must be in Him and not in our circumstances.

The fear of man brings a snare, But he who trusts in the LORD will be exalted (Prov. 29:25).

Fear hindered me most of my life. I remember going to summer camp as a child and being afraid of heights. One year there was a trip to a forest tower for the young campers. After climbing about four or five steps up the tower, I carefully backed down to the ground. Fear of heights seemed to follow me everyplace I went.

THE LORD HAS MADE A WAY FOR US TO BE DELIVERED FROM FEAR, BUT OUR TRUST MUST BE IN HIM AND NOT IN OUR CIRCUMSTANCES.

The fear did not change after I became an adult. One summer Dale, our children and I agreed to move a missionary family to Mexico. We were given a homemade trailer to pull behind our car from East Texas to Guadalajara, Mexico. Because the trailer was not built properly, it caused a severe wavering to occur when the car reached speeds over 45 miles per hour. Much of the trip inside Mexico would be through high mountains, with steep cliffs and narrow roads with no shoulders. Just the thought of the trip brought me fear.

After several days of travel, with my stomach feeling queasy and my knuckles white from a combination of holding on tight and much prayer, we reached a very high place in the mountains named Zacatecas. "If you think this is bad, wait until tomorrow," someone said. "Tomorrow will be the worst part of the trip." All night I tossed in my bed, dreading the next day. All I could do was pray. And pray I did.

As we drove out of the motel parking lot the next morning, I picked up my Bible. It opened to Psalm 91, and I began to read aloud:

> He who dwells in the shelter of the Most High Will abide in the shadow of the Almighty. I will say to the LORD, "My refuge and my fortress, My God, in whom I trust!" (Ps. 91:1,2).

Tears started to flow, and my voice choked as I laid the Bible on the seat. "Lord, if You don't deliver me from this fear," I silently prayed, "I don't know what I will do. I have prayed, meditated on Your Word and done everything I know to do. Only You can set me free. I put my trust in You." As I closed my eyes and leaned back on the seat, I seemed to fall into Jesus' arms. He became my refuge and high tower in the midst of the gripping fear.

After about 15 minutes of basking in the presence of the Lord, I felt something break off and lift from me. Immediately, I sat straight up in the car and looked out the window. Across the mountains were waterfalls cascading down the side of the slopes. They were beautiful! And the mountains—how majestic, how awesome! The Creator had made these mountains so glorious for His people to enjoy. Fear had robbed me from enjoying the Lord's creation. What had brought terror to my heart a few minutes earlier became a place of rejoicing and thanksgiving. I was now free for the first time in my life.

Each time I climb into a plane or ride in a glassed-in elevator, I am reminded of the Lord's mercy in setting me free from fear.

Today, without harassment of fear, I can enjoy prayer walks in high places or participate in prayer endeavors for cities and nations. The Lord is faithful! Fear will keep us from being sharp in the spirit. Fear is an enemy to drain the believer of strength for the battle.

STRONG FAITH

Another means of sharpening our spiritual senses is to develop a life of strong faith. Faith simply means *being persuaded* or *belief.* Everything we do in the kingdom of God must be done in faith. When we are born again, it is faith in the finished work of the Cross that gives us the assurance of salvation. We must be persuaded that when we pray, God will answer. Unbelief will keep us from hearing and obeying in intercession. Prayer then becomes a religious ritual without the power to receive answers from heaven. Faith is a necessary ingredient in supernatural ministry:

> Trust will lie down in the boat, but faith will speak to the storms, winds and mountains of life.[3]

DRESSED FOR SUCCESS

After we have allowed the Lord to cleanse us of anything that would defile our hearts or lives, after we resist every form of fear and after we embrace faith for intercession, one more step must be taken. We need the proper clothing. The clothing must be properly fitted to each of us. This clothing cannot be designed for someone else. Often we see others who appear so powerful in intercession. They seem to get answers to their prayers. We try praying the way they pray, but it doesn't work the same. Why? The Lord may have fit other people for different tasks. You may not be called to the same task. That does not mean your assignment is any less important—just different. Wear the mantle designed for you—do the job assigned to you—so that you will be victorious in battle.

As a young man, David understood this principle:

> Then Saul clothed David with his garments and put a bronze helmet on his head, and he clothed him with armor. And David girded his sword over his armor and tried to walk, for he had not tested them. So David said to Saul, "I cannot go with these, for I have not tested them." And David took them off (1 Sam. 17:38,39).

Every intercessor is in a different season, or time of spiritual life, with a different degree of spiritual growth. Each one is valuable in the Kingdom. Each has been given a task from God to accomplish. Don't allow intimidation or comparison to keep you from taking your place in the Lord's army. David could not wear Saul's armor—it just didn't fit. So he took it off and wore his own. Even though he was just a young man, he was able to defeat the giant Goliath, who had brought fear into the hearts of Saul's well-trained army.

A SHARP BATTLE AX

As we allow the Lord to sharpen our spiritual ax, we will gain perception and strength for the battle. The strength will keep our ears tuned to the voice of the Lord. It will cause our eyes to see where the enemy is and know how to direct our prayers. Spiritual strength will release our hearts to be obedient to the Lord. Less effort in battle and more frequent breakthroughs will occur. Sharpen your ax and see victories as a result of your intercession.

QUESTIONS FOR CONSIDERATION:

1. Have you ever become weary from extended periods of intercession? discouraged? downhearted? What did you do?
2. Describe a time in your life when the Lord convicted you about a condition of "dullness."
3. What did you do to change your condition of dullness?
4. Have you had your daily spiritual bath today?
5. Are there areas of fear that still trouble you? Have you ever experienced deliverance from any of your fears?
6. Have you ever tried to wear someone else's armor or mantle? What happened?
7. What are some of the dangers of an intercessor when he becomes "dull"?

Chapter Four

HEARING GOD BRINGS BREAKTHROUGH

Then the LORD came and stood and called as at other times, "Samuel! Samuel!" And Samuel said, "Speak, for Thy servant is listening."

1 SAMUEL 3:10

Excitedly, I entered the home of my new friend. She seemed to be such a "spiritual giant," and I had just come into a new experience with the Holy Spirit. Although I had been a Christian since the age of 12, I really didn't know anything about this spirit-filled walk. However, I was eager to learn anything and everything I could.

HE SPEAKS TO PEOPLE TODAY

The first words out of Mary's mouth proved how little I knew of the spirit-filled life: "The Lord spoke to me and told me to go on a 'no pleasant bread' fast," she stated.

All I could do was pray a silent prayer of relief to the Lord. "Father, I am so glad you didn't say that to me. The first reason is because I didn't know You could talk to people today. The next reason is I don't have a clue as to what a 'no pleasant bread' fast is." Immediately, my mind was flooded with questions.

Does God really talk to people today?

How can I be sure it is the Lord speaking?

In what ways does He speak?

What did Mary mean by a "no pleasant bread fast"?

Will I ever be able to hear the Lord as clearly as my friend?

Does God talk to all Christians or only to select ones?

I had attended a traditional church from the time I was a small child. Jesus became my personal Lord and Savior when I was 12, and I was a faithful church member all my life. Now as an adult, I was hearing things about the Holy Spirit I had never heard. In fact, the teachings from my church told me that God does not speak to His people today. Not often, that is. And then He only speaks in one way. I remember the discourse so well: "If you are reading the Bible and a Scripture seems to lift off the page and grab your heart, then God is speaking to you. Otherwise, He does not speak. He spoke to people in the times of the Bible, but we live in a different time. He has given us the Bible and does not need to speak to us today."

WE ARE THE SHEEP WHO HEAR HIS VOICE

Were all these well-educated ministers wrong? Mary seemed so confident that it was the Lord who had spoken to her. The conflict in my mind sent me searching the Scriptures to uncover answers to my questions. I soon discovered that the Bible clearly states God's desire and promise to speak to His children:

> My sheep hear My voice, and I know them, and they follow Me (John 10:27).

We are called the sheep of His pasture and have the privilege of hearing the voice of the Good Shepherd. What a promise! God is not so busy holding stars in space, keeping galaxies on their course or causing this earth to spin on its axis that He doesn't have time to talk to you and me. He even gives us the assurance that we will know the difference between His voice and other voices that may speak to us.

> And a stranger they simply will not follow, but will flee from him, because they do not know the voice of strangers (John 10:5).

While searching the Scriptures, I realized that a "no pleasant bread fast" is a type of abstinence Daniel practiced while an official in the court of the Persian King Cyrus (see Dan. 10:1-3). The results of the fast, combined with a lifetime of obedience to God, yielded great prophetic and spiritual insight.

Intercessors should be able to hear God speak. As He speaks, He will reveal areas that need prayer, strategies to overcome the enemy, actions or declarations to break the power of hindrance, and even reveal the sources of warfare. Victory can be obtained through obedience to the Word of the Lord.

Several years ago Dale and I were part of a citywide pastors' prayer meeting. After praying for about 15 minutes, my attention was drawn to another pastor in the room. I had never seen him before and didn't know anything about him. As my eyes fastened on him, the Lord began to speak to me about him. I did not expect this. I had come with my husband to pray. The group was not used to women speaking up, and I wanted to be a quiet pastor's wife. *Lord, please tell this to one of the men pastors. I want to be obedient, but I don't want to tell this pastor what You are saying.* My begging God didn't make any difference. He just kept speaking and gently nudging me to be obedient.

At the end of the prayer session, time was given for sharing anything the pastors felt God was saying. One after another shared. I kept waiting. Surely, someone had heard the Lord concerning the pastor the Lord had spoken to me about. However, no one even addressed the matter. "Is there anyone else who has heard something from the Lord?" the leader asked. After much hesitation, I indicated I needed to give a "word" to the new pastor. Permission was granted, and I began.

"You are in the midst of a great conflict in your church," I said. "God has granted you an incredible gift of mercy, and the mercy is overriding the wisdom He has for you in this situation. There is a man in your church who is involved in the finances of the church, and he is causing problems." At that moment the pastor pulled a big handkerchief from his pocket, put his face in it and sobbed so loudly it was hard to hear what I was saying.

"The Lord says you need to deal with the situation," I went on, "because it is affecting your whole church. You already know what to do, but you have been hesitant because of your mercy. If you will be obedient to the Lord, healing and restoration will come to your church. The finances will change, and you will have more than enough to meet the needs."

Quickly, I sat down in my chair as the pastor continued to sob for several minutes. Months later I met the pastor while shopping in a local grocery store. "Barbara, I have to tell you what happened. When you spoke the word to me at the prayer meeting, I knew who you were talking about. God had already been dealing with me about the situation, but I did not want to confront it. I did what the Lord said, and now our church has experienced a breakthrough. There is peace for the first time, and our offerings have increased greatly." As I thanked him for sharing the story with me, I also prayed, *Lord, teach me how to hear You more and more in times of intercession.*

In this situation the Lord had spoken to me through a still, small voice. It is the most frequent way the Lord speaks to His people. He spoke to Elijah in the same way:

So He said, "Go forth, and stand on the mountain before the LORD." And behold, the LORD was passing by! And a great and strong wind was rending the mountains and breaking in pieces the rocks before the LORD; but the LORD was not in the wind. And after the wind an earthquake, but the LORD was not in the earthquake. And after the earthquake a fire, but the LORD was not in the fire; and after the fire a sound of a gentle blowing ["a still small voice," *KJV*]. And it came about when Elijah heard it, that he wrapped his face in his mantle, and went out and stood in the entrance of the cave. And behold, a voice came to him and said, "What are you doing here, Elijah?" (1 Kings 19:11-13).

GOD'S OTHER SPEAKING METHODS

Are there other ways God can speak and bring similar breakthroughs? If hearing the Lord made such a difference in the life of the pastor's church, what else can it do? What are some other ways He speaks?

DREAMS

Throughout the Bible, there are times when God spoke to His people through dreams. There are times when I know the Lord is speaking to me through a dream. Other times, I know the dream is a result of a very busy day or unresolved conflict in my mind. Often when the Lord speaks to me in a dream, it is still vivid when I am awake. Dreams I received from the Lord many years ago are still explicit today. God communicates many times to intercessors through dreams. Author Jane Hamon says these dreams are sometimes used to communicate battle plans to the intercessors:

It has been amazing to me as copastor of a prophetic church when several people in the body, and at times even people who live in another place, have extremely similar troubling dreams. They have, at times, brought them to me because of their disturbing nature only to discover that several others have had similar dreams within a short period of time. Many times these dreams provide revelation concerning our heavenly battle.

Again, prayer is the key to properly responding to such dreams or visions. God is raising up intercessors around the world who are becoming more and more armed to God's revelations and are ready in an instant to organize and do battle through prayer.

These prophetic prayer warriors call upon God for His divine angelic assistance as did Daniel when battling the Prince of Persia (see Dan. 10:13). Many times the plans revealed through the dream will enable intercessors to avoid natural disasters such as storms or earthquakes. Some have told of dreaming of destructive storms sweeping through their towns and leveling it flat. As the storm actually began to hit the next day, their prayers prevailed and damage was minimal.[1]

The prophet Joel spoke of a time when God would speak to His people through dreams and visions:

And it will come about after this that I will pour out My Spirit on all mankind; and your sons and daughters will prophesy, Your old men will dream dreams, your young men will see visions. And even on the male and female servants I will pour out My Spirit in those days (Joel 2:28,29).

VISIONS

A vision is like a dream except that you are awake when it occurs. Peter's commission to eat with and minister to the Gentiles came in a vision (see Acts 10:9-23). Dr. C. Peter Wagner reveals the importance of this type of communication from God:

> God knew that ordinary communication processes would not be adequate to move Peter in the radical direction He wanted him to go. So God did an extraordinary thing and gave Peter the famous vision of the unclean food in the sheet. Peter's background had personally prepared him to receive visions. For one thing, it would fit his worldview. Unlike many today, Peter believed that one of God's normal ways of communicating from time to time was through visions and dreams. He was praying at the time, so his heart was open to God.[2]

AUDIBLE VOICE

Prayer opens our spirits to be able to hear God more clearly. There are times when the voice of God in intercession can mean life or death. Sometimes the Lord will even speak in an audible voice. Communication from God in an audible voice is not frequent, but it does happen. My friend Carol Cartwright heard the Lord speak to her audibly when she was in a critical situation.

Carol's son Gary was only two years old. The doctors had given a diagnosis of polio several months prior, and now Gary was in critical condition. Carol held the small child in her arms and silently prayed that anxious morning in the hospital room. While she was still praying, the doctors entered the room. Immediately after they came into the room, the baby died in his mother's arms. Following normal medical protocol, they examined the dead baby and reached to take him from his mother. At that moment, Carol heard the Lord speak to her in an audible voice: "He shall not die! He shall not die! He shall not die!"

Carol cried, "No!" Thinking she was just a hysterical mother, everyone left the room to give her a few more minutes to hold the body of her dead baby.

Carol knew the Lord had spoken to her in an audible voice, and she continued to hold her baby, waiting for the miracle. About half an hour later, the baby's body shook. He opened his eyes and life was restored. Breakthrough had occurred. Today Gary is an adult with a child of his own. God had spoken in an audible voice even though others in the room did not hear. The same thing happened during the life of Jesus:

> "Father, glorify your name!" Then a voice came from heaven, "I have glorified it, and will glorify it again." The crowd that was there and heard it said it had thundered; others said an angel had spoken to him (John 12:28,29, *NIV*).

THROUGH THE SCRIPTURES

Although God can speak in a very dramatic way, such as an audible voice, He can also speak in a less sensational but just as genuine way through the Scriptures. In fact, when we believe He has spoken to us, the word should always be judged by the Scriptures. He will *never* speak contrary to His Word.

The Scriptures give strength to us in the same way physical food energizes us. It gives light to guide us as we walk with the Lord:

> Thy word is a lamp to my feet, and a light to my path (Ps. 119:105).

There are times in prayer when the Lord will use the Scriptures to instruct us and give wisdom in a situation we are facing. Herman Riffel says in his book, *Learning to Hear God's Voice*:

> It was early in the summer of 1970 in Zurich, Switzerland. Lillie and I had been asked by missionaries from ten countries to come and minister to them. When I asked them about the dates they would like us to come, they suggested I set up the schedule the way it suited us. But how could I arrange a schedule to speak to groups of missionaries who are often away from their homes in tribal areas for months at a time? It would be impossible to arrive at the right time in all ten countries. At least it seemed so.
>
> While I was puzzling over the schedule, a verse of Scripture kept repeating itself to me: "I will go before thee, and make the crooked places straight" (Isa. 45:2, *KJV*). That phrase kept going through my mind almost like a ringing in my ears. In two hours the agent and I had set up a 'round-the-world tour including all the cities that I had asked for. That schedule never needed to be changed.[3]

THROUGH SPIRITUAL GIFTINGS

The Lord also speaks to us through the gifts of the Holy Spirit and through other people. God spoke to the apostle Paul through another person:

> After we had been there a number of days, a prophet named Agabus came down from Judea. Coming over to us, he took Paul's belt, tied his own hands and feet with it and said, "The Holy Spirit says, 'In this way the Jews of Jerusalem will bind the owner of this belt and will hand him over to the Gentiles'" (Acts 21:10,11, *NIV*).

Many times I have had prophets or those who operated in the gifts of the Holy Spirit speak a word from the Lord to me. These words have helped me in making decisions, kept me from making mistakes and brought tremendous strength when I needed it. I have also found the Lord speaks to me through many other ways as I am praying and listening for His voice.

Many years ago I was president of a local Women's Aglow chapter. The group had increased greatly in numbers. We could no longer get all the women in the meeting room. I knew the Lord had the best place and would direct me if I would be sensitive to Him.

GOD WILL SPEAK TO YOU IF YOU WILL LET HIM. YOUR HEARING, HOWEVER, MUST BE TESTED—BY THE WORD.

After praying for several weeks, there seemed to be an answer. A hotel had a room that seemed perfect. All the women on the board agreed. The advisors felt it was the right place. As I drove over to the hotel to sign the contract, I continued to pray. "Lord, please speak to me. Let me know if I am making the right decision. Everyone else thinks this place is right for our group. I want to know if *You* say it is right."

As I pulled into the parking lot of the hotel, which was across the street from a church, I saw the church sign: "Oh ye of little faith, why do you doubt?" I knew I had the answer! To me, it was the voice of the Lord speaking direction into my life! The group continued to increase until we eventually filled that room and had to move again.

God wants to be involved in all the affairs of our lives. He will guide and direct us by speaking to us if we will let Him. His voice can keep us from making a lot of mistakes. It can keep us on a straight path. Our hearing, however, must be tested.

AN IMPORTANT CAUTION

I remember a man who lived in a town where I once lived. He and his wife were leading a young people's group. Revival among teenagers was taking place. The Lord was setting kids free from drugs, alcohol and every evil thing. One day the man came home and announced to his wife, "The Lord told me to leave you and marry someone else." She believed him. Within a short time, the man left his wife and moved in with the other woman. Soon, he left that woman and moved in with another woman. This pattern continued over a period of years. Naturally, the revival among the young people died out. Many walked away from the Lord due to their confusion and disappointment in their leader. What happened?

What had seemed to be a word from the Lord had not been tested by the Scripture. Deception from the enemy came to stop the work of the Holy Spirit. Since the married couple was not accountable to anyone, no one could speak into their lives. Although God speaks to His people today, such words need to be tested.

THE NEED FOR ACCOUNTABILITY

The nature of our hearing is imperfect. We don't even hear others clearly. Spiritual leaders are given to the Body of Christ to watch over us and help us grow:

> Obey your leaders and submit to their authority. They keep watch over you as men who must give an account. Obey them so that their work will be a joy, not a burden, for that would be of no advantage to you (Heb. 13:17, *NIV*).

Intercessors get in trouble when they develop an independent spirit and get out from under a spiritual covering or protection. No person, including leaders, is above accountability. Each of us needs a submissive spirit and the protection of others to speak into our lives. Cindy Jacobs shares her own experience concerning submission to authority in her book, *The Voice of God*:

> When I received my call to ministry from the Lord, the subject of authority was heavy on my heart. One day in prayer the Holy Spirit cautioned me, "Cindy, if you want to move in great authority, you must be subject to others in authority. Your anointing will grow in proportion to your understanding of spiritual submission. Remember the centurion who came to Jesus and asked Him to heal his servant boy. A great miracle occurred because he understood authority."[4]

PRECAUTIONS

I have been involved in many situations for the purpose of reconciling intercessors and pastors. Several pastors have reported confusion, disunity and pain due to intercessors who felt they had "the word of the Lord" for the church but would not submit to the counsel of leadership. The Lord is bringing healing to those divisions. Several precautions can help prevent separations between intercessors and pastors.

A DESIRE DOES NOT CONSTITUTE A WORD FROM GOD

The first precaution is to avoid trying to change the vision of the church. Intercessors may see something in another church or in a conference and then decide it needs to happen in their own church. Learn the difference between the voice of your own human spirit and the voice of the Lord. Accept the fact that it is a desire you have, but that it is not necessarily for your church or leaders, even if it is a godly desire and in line with what the Lord is doing today.

GOD'S TIMING

Another area of hearing God involves the timing for fulfillment. Be willing to wait on God. Remember that God promised Abraham a son who would come forth from his own body (see Gen. 15:4). Yet it was 25 years later before Isaac was born. Often we are ready before the Lord is ready. I have heard my pastor say, "Lord, you have never been late, but you have missed a lot of good opportunities to be early." Intercessors can only pray and stand in faith for the Lord to fulfill His Word. During this season, we should let the fruit of patience be worked in our lives. The Word of the Lord will stand the test of time.

As a child, the prophet Samuel did not distinguish the Lord's voice when he first began to hear Him speak. It took encouragement from Eli the priest and years of walking with God to help him recognize when God was speaking. Samuel was faithful and the Scriptures speak of God's faithfulness to validate Samuel:

The LORD was with Samuel as he grew up, and he let none of his words fall to the ground (1 Sam. 3:19, *NIV*).

THANKFUL FOR GOD'S VOICE TODAY

I am thankful God speaks to His people today. In times of intercession, we need to hear what the Lord wants us to pray. We need to know how we should pray to get powerful results. As the Lord opens our spiritual ears, we are able to pray the prayers that change individual lives. We are able to pray the prayers that change cities and nations.

QUESTIONS FOR CONSIDERATION:

1. Describe several ways you have heard God speak to you.
2. How did you test the word you heard?
3. What is the usual way you hear God speak?
4. Have any of your words "fallen to the ground"? What happened?
5. To whom do you look for spiritual accountability?
6. Do you consider patience an abundant fruit in your life?

Chapter Five

MAN BECOMES GOD'S VOICE FOR BREAKTHROUGH

The voice of the LORD is upon the waters; The God of glory thunders, The LORD is over many waters.

PSALM 29:3

"It was the most powerful prayer meeting I have ever attended," my friend Elizabeth Alves proclaimed with great excitement. She had just left a prayer meeting held on September 22, 1989 in Europe. As president of the Executive Board for Intercessors International, she was sharing about the breakthrough. Leaders of major intercession ministries had gathered together in Europe to pray and receive strategy from the Lord.

"Everyone had such a feeling in the Lord that it was a significant conference," Elizabeth told us. "Even the brochure for the conference had a wall with water breaking through it.

"It was a time after intense worship. As Kjell Kjoberg stood up to speak, the Lord spoke to me and said I would hear a word that would change history.

"Kjell came out with a booming voice, 'Lord, I come to You like Moses. I bring every prayer that has ever been prayed since the inception. I stand spiritually before the wall of Hungary and I say, "Let My people go!" Next, I bring the prayers of the people. I stand in the center of Prague, Czechoslovakia. As Jesus said to the man who was deaf, I say to the wall, "Be opened in Jesus' name." So we can know this is you, Lord, let it be done within the

next seven weeks. Lord, so we know this is You, let us see the statue of Lenin being carried out on the shoulders of men for the
world to see.'"

Such a bold prayer—such a strong request of God!

As I listened to this story, I wondered, *Does God answer prayers
like this? Can a man through prayer demand that people in other places
be set free for God's purposes? Do all intercessors have the same kind of
authority? After all, isn't God sovereign, doing what He wills?*

PRAYING DOWN WALLS AND RULERS

Elizabeth went on to explain. It seems that, in a short time, the
story of the fall of the governmental walls of Hungary and
Czechoslovakia was in the newspapers. Another man, Bert
Holdbecker, leader of Intercessory Prayer for Germany, stood up.
Bert prayed for Romania and called down the fall of Ceaucescu,
that his reign would cease before the end of the year. Ceaucescu
was the dictator in Romania who was more ruthless than Stalin.
He was murdered in December.

Elizabeth also prayed and called out for the government of
East Germany to fall. She asked the Lord to release His power
and for Communism to fall and lose its power. On November 8
(American date—the date is different in Germany because they
are one day different from America) the wall came down, first in
Hungary. Then on November 9 the wall came down in
Czechoslovakia.

*What did this prayer meeting that our president of Intercessors
International participated in have to do with these walls falling? Did this
happen because these were such powerful intercessors? Does God use
strong prayer warriors for special assignments and ordinary people for
less important undertakings? Could God possibly use me to help change
the world?*

I did not fully comprehend the spiritual dynamics of what had happened, but the story stuck in my mind. I could not forget it. Maybe God could use His people in ways I had never dreamed possible. I determined to study and pray to discover the Lord's will for His people.

GOD'S ETERNAL PLAN

One of the first things I discovered was that God has always had a plan for the world and for our individual lives. He is not like many people today, who simply take each day as it comes without considering the future. The Church has also been guilty of keeping its focus solely on getting out of "this old evil world" rather than helping us discover why we are here. God's plan for man is stated at the beginning of the Bible:

> Then God said, "Let Us make man in Our image, according to Our likeness; and let them rule over the fish of the sea and over the birds of the sky and over the cattle and over all the earth, and over every creeping thing that creeps on the earth." And God created man in His own image, in the image of God He created him; male and female He created them. And God blessed them; and God said to them, "Be fruitful and multiply, and fill the earth, and subdue it; and rule over the fish of the sea and over the birds of the sky, and over every living thing that moves on the earth" (Gen. 1:26-28).

God made man in His own image and likeness. After the creation of all the other creatures, He created man in the nearest resemblance to Himself, more than any of the other creatures. Only Jesus is the *express* image of God, yet God chose to make man similar to Himself. He simply put some of His honor upon man. In man, God brought together flesh and spirit, heaven and earth.

God's man is to be His representative in the earth. As His ambassador, man has been given delegated authority and dominion in the earth. Dutch Sheets explains the meaning of Genesis 1:26-28 in his book *Intercessory Prayer*:

> Adam was comparable to or similar to God—so much like God that it was illusionary. God was recognized in Adam, which meant that Adam "carried the weight" here on earth. Adam represented God, presenting again His will on the earth. Adam was God's governor or manager here. The earth was Adam's assignment—it was under Adam's charge or care. Adam was the watchman or guardian. How things went on planet Earth, for better or worse, depended on Adam and his offspring.[1]

Adam, as God's representative, would display God's character and authority as well as be God's voice or mouthpiece in the earth. Adam and Eve would speak for God to the earth and its inhabitants. They would speak in the same way that a United States ambassador speaks for the president of our country to the people to whom he is sent.

As God's representative, however, Adam and Eve failed to fulfill God's plan for them in the earth. Genesis 3 gives the historical account of the fall. Adam and Eve consciously and deliberately violated God's explicit and emphatic command by eating of the forbidden fruit. As a result of the fall, we gave up God's plan to subdue the earth. There was now a place of separation between God and humans.

Restoration

After the Fall, God in His mercy promised Adam and Eve redemption and restoration. He gave them garments to cover their nakedness, and He promised that the woman's Seed would one day break the serpent's head. This promise spoke of Jesus:

> So then as through one transgression there resulted condemnation to all men, even so through one act of righteousness there resulted justification of life to all men. For as through the one man's disobedience the many were made sinners, even so through the obedience of the One the many will be made righteous (Rom. 5:18,19).

Jesus came to inaugurate the new covenant. God works in the earth through covenant. Adam and Eve broke covenant with God, but through Jesus a way was made for restoration. Through the new birth, man becomes a covenant partner with the Lord. Intercessors, as God's covenant partners, are those today who stand in the gaps or breaches that separate people from God. They are those who participate with God in redeeming the earth.

The prophet Ezekiel spoke of God's burden for a man who would stand in the gap for the restoration that would come to individuals, cities and nations:

> And I searched for a man among them who should build up the wall and stand in the gap before Me for the land, that I should not destroy it; but I found no one (Ezek. 22:30).

STANDING IN THE GAP

The words "gap" and "breach" have the same meaning. When a wall was broken or breached by an attacking army, there was danger for those repairing the gap. The Bible speaks of false prophets who were nowhere to be found when it was time to repair the wall. The true prophets were identified so closely with God's people that they were willing to expose themselves to danger to see the wall repaired. Moses was willing to stand in the gap for God's people (see Ps. 106:23). However, Jesus was the only one worthy to pay the price through His death, burial and resurrection, and to stand in the gap and repair the wall separating God and man. Because of what He did, He bought back what man had given away. Jesus then restored humanity's legal authority to be God's representatives on earth, so God's plan for man would ultimately be fulfilled. Man could once again rule through the Messiah, Jesus. The Lord extends His goodness into all nations, because His people participate with the Lord in redeeming the earth. His representative would be the one Ezekiel said God looked for to stand in the gaps or breaches.

> YOU AND I WILL BE THE VOICE OF
> THE LORD TO HELP BRING HEALING
> TO THE EARTH.

Webster defines "breach" as a "breaking or being broken open; failure to observe the terms as of a law or promise; violation; infraction; an opening made by a breakthrough, as in a wall or line of defense; a broken or torn place."[2]

The Lord today is raising up intercessors who will stand in the gaps to intercede. As God's covenant partners, they will become the voice of the Lord in the earth to speak forgiveness, healing and restoration to the broken places needing repair. He is looking for those who are in covenant with Him. That means you and me. We will be the voice of the Lord to help bring healing to the earth.

> And those from among you will rebuild the ancient ruins; You will raise up the age-old foundations; And you will be called the repairer of the breach, The restorer of the streets in which to dwell (Isa. 58:12).

As the people of God, we stand in the gap, and we have the ability to be used by God as His voice to speak words inspired by the power of the Holy Spirit. Psalm 29 speaks of the many things the voice of the Lord accomplishes:

> The voice of the LORD is upon the waters; The God of glory thunders, The LORD is over many waters. The voice of the LORD is powerful, The voice of the LORD is majestic. The voice of the LORD breaks the cedars; Yes, the LORD breaks in pieces the cedars of Lebanon. And He makes Lebanon skip like a calf, And Sirion like a young wild ox. The voice of the LORD hews out flames of fire. The voice of the LORD shakes the wilderness; The LORD shakes the wilderness of Kadesh. The voice of the LORD makes the deer to calve, And strips the forests bare, And in His temple everything says, "Glory!" (vv. 3-9).

THE LORD'S POWER IN OUR WORDS

Since we are the voice of the Lord in the earth, God has placed His power in our words to accomplish great things. God's Spirit flowing through us is like a river, as described in John 7:

He who believes in Me, as the Scripture said, "From his innermost being shall flow rivers of living water." But this He spoke of the Spirit (vv. 38,39).

The rivers of living water provide a means of release for the voice of the Lord to be able to flow. According to Psalm 29, His voice is upon the waters. His voice then is upon the rivers of living water flowing from the mouths of intercessors. Dutch Sheets says:

After rebuking the storm, Jesus rebuked the disciples for their fear and unbelief, implying that they should have rebuked it. He also followed up His cursing of the fig tree with a promise that we could speak to mountains and cast them into the sea. He is describing the power of the Holy Spirit-inspired declaration. We become the voice of God upon the earth.[3]

Several things are listed in Psalm 29 describing what the voice of the Lord does. One of the things mentioned is that the voice of the Lord breaks. Spiros Zodhiates gives powerful examples of the Hebrew word for break, which is *shabar*:

To burst, to break into pieces; to rend; to tear in pieces (like a wild bear); To destroy, to perish (such as a kingdom, a city, or a people); To be broken by penitence (i.e., to be contrite); To cause to break forth, to open (the womb, i.e., the infant appears).[4]

Looking at the definitions of *shabar*, it is easy to see how the voice of the Lord through intercessors can help destroy the works of evil and release brokenness and repentance to those not walking with the Lord. The voice of the Lord through His people also "opens the womb," so to speak, for the Lord to "birth" His purposes in the earth.

When Moses came down from the mountain and saw his people involved in an orgy, he "shattered" (*shabar*) the tablets of the Law (see Exod. 32:19). Altars of false gods were many times the victims of *shabar* (see 2 Kings 18:4; 23:14; 2 Chron. 34:4). These examples are good pictures of what happens to the works of darkness as God's representatives, through intercession, release God's voice upon the waters. But shattering the works of darkness is only one thing the voice of the Lord does.

God's voice also shakes. The Hebrew word for shake is *chuwl*. Some meanings of *chuwl* are:

> To be afraid; to tremble with pain, to be terrified; to be in labor (of childbirth), to bear a child; to produce, to cause to bring forth.[5]

The voice of the Lord causes the enemy to be afraid. It causes him to be so terrified that he will tremble with pain. God's voice also causes the words spoken to produce and bring forth. His voice births the fruit of our labors. I am convinced that if we could see into the realm of the spirit, we would pray more. Often we pray, but because we don't see an immediate answer, we think nothing has happened. Remember, it took 21 days for the answer to come to Daniel (see Dan. 10:12,13). Sometimes it will take even more time before we see the results of our intercession.

A CITY RELEASED FROM OPPRESSION

Several years ago I had been asked to speak at a conference in a large city. When I arrived I sensed a strong spiritual oppression in that place. "Why is there oppression in this city?" I asked the

Lord. It looked like such a beautiful place. The city had a reputation for music and rejoicing. After praying, I felt a need to teach on spiritual warfare. During those years, warfare was not a popular topic. While talking to the worship leader over the phone, I asked her to lead us in warfare songs that evening. Little did I know what the Lord was about to do!

When I arrived at the meeting that night, someone came to me and excitedly told me about the city. A new building had recently been completed and the dedication for the building held the previous week. Some of the Christians in the city had participated in the ceremony. The building was called a "Parthenon." Around the top of the building were carvings of a number of false gods.

The dedication ceremony included dedicating the music of the city to "the gods." I knew then why the oppression was there. God's covenant had been broken and a false covenant established with "the gods."

That night at the conference, we corporately confessed and repented of our sin as Christians for participating in a false covenant. We broke the power of that covenant and asked the Lord to restore His covenant with us.

Afterward, we faced in the direction of the Parthenon and spoke as the voice of the Lord: "We command every false god to crumble. You must come down. We declare that Jesus is Lord over this city, and we now dedicate the music of this city to Him. He is the creator of music, and music belongs to Him." Later, some of the intercessors attending the meeting walked around the Parthenon as they continued praying.

Six months later I was at a conference in another state. The worship leader from the city with the Parthenon was also at this conference. "Barbara, I have to tell you what happened," she said. "The gods around the top of the Parthenon are falling. In fact, the city officials have put guardrails around the bottom.

The architects are confused. They can't understand why the Parthenon in Greece has stood for several hundred years. Now this one is crumbling after only six months."

Although we did spiritual warfare at the meeting, we didn't realize how powerful the voice of the Lord was! Our intention was not to destroy a building but to "cause to perish," to "break in pieces," the works of the enemy. Our desire was to "cause to bring forth" and to "produce" the will of the Lord for that city. Today God is using music from that city to bless the Body of Christ, and those who hear the music say, "Glory!"

A TIME TO BE THE LORD'S VOICE

How many times have you heard someone say, "God will do what He wants whenever He wants to"? The statement is only partially true. There is a right time for all things to be done (see Eccles. 3:1). The Lord will give His intercessors an "Issachar anointing" (see chapter 2 of this book) to know times and seasons so we will know what we are to do (see 1 Chron. 12:32). Many times He is ready for something to be done, but He needs someone to pray for His will to be done. He will put His words in the mouths of intercessors when He is ready to perform His Word:

> Then the LORD stretched out His hand and touched my mouth, and the LORD said to me, "Behold, I have put My words in your mouth. See, I have appointed you this day over the nations and over the kingdoms, to pluck up and to break down, to destroy and to overthrow, to build and to plant."
>
> And the word of the LORD came to me saying, "What do you see, Jeremiah?" And I said, "I see a rod of an almond tree." Then the Lord said to me, "You have seen well, for I am watching over My word to perform it" (Jer. 1:9-12).

The Hebrew word for "watching" is *shaqad*. The word means waking or to be sleepless, alert or vigilant.[6]

God is awake. He is sleepless. He is alert and vigilant to hasten the performance of the words He has placed in our mouths. God showed Jeremiah an almond tree. Why did He do that? The word almond is close to the spelling of *shaqad*. The Hebrew word for almond is *shaqed*. Of all trees, the almond tree blossoms the earliest. In Hebrew thought the almond tree is considered the "waker." God gave Jeremiah a picture to illustrate how ready, alert, sleepless and vigilant He is to perform His Word. In the same way that the almond tree is considered the "waker" tree, God is awake and will bring to pass the words into the mouths of His servants.

Let the Lord use you as His voice. Don't allow the enemy to intimidate you. Let the Spirit of the Lord flow through you. You will see God's enemies put to flight.

QUESTIONS FOR CONSIDERATION:

1. How does my praying affect people in other nations?
2. What is God's plan for His people?
3. Since the earth is full of evil, shouldn't we just try to make it through life without being entangled in the affairs of the world? If not, why not?
4. What are some breaches in my life or in the city where I live?
5. Describe the connection between "rivers of living water" (John 7:38) and "the voice of the Lord is upon the waters" (Ps. 29:3).
6. Have you released the living waters to flow through you today?

Chapter Six

PROPHETIC INTERCESSION

After these things I looked, and behold, a door standing open in heaven,
and the first voice which I had heard, like the sound of a trumpet
speaking with me, said, "Come up here, and I will show you what
must take place after these things."

REVELATION 4:1

Brenda Ramsey had spent several months seeking the Lord for the baptism of the Holy Spirit. During the summer of 1985, she was scheduled to attend a Christian conference that included about 1,000 people in Estes Park, Colorado. In preparing to go, she prayed for the Lord to send someone to lay hands on her to be filled with the Holy Spirit and to receive her prayer language. She was confident the Lord would bring someone across her path to give her what her heart desired.

Brenda attended the conference with her daughter, Tiffany. James, Brenda's husband, and his friend planned to drive to Colorado from Texas and meet them at the end of the week.

On Thursday, during the conference, Brenda met a lady named Mary. Mary told her how she loved to pray for people to receive their prayer language. Brenda was thrilled at the connection with this new friend and asked her to come to her room and pray. The Lord showed up in power! When Mary laid hands on Brenda, she fell to the floor under the power of the Holy Spirit as she received her prayer language. Brenda's daughter, Tiffany, came into the room during this time. When Brenda laid her hands on Tiffany, she also received the fullness of the Spirit.

That night Brenda went to bed, prayed and fell asleep. At 3:00 A.M. she found herself sitting straight up in bed as though she had never been asleep. Immediately she asked the Lord why she was sitting up and wide awake. The only impression she had was to pray. She got out of the bed and began praying in her new prayer language, as she remembered 1 Corinthians 14:14: "For if I pray in a tongue, my spirit prays, but my mind is unfruitful." Brenda continued to pray for a while. After she sensed the crisis was over, whatever it was, she got back into bed and fell asleep.

Brenda did not learn until later the impact her prayers had made. James and his friend had left Texas after they got off work on Thursday afternoon. Each man took turns driving non-stop throughout the night.

Brenda's husband and his friend arrived in Colorado on Friday. The friend then told Brenda about what happened the night before.

"I woke up when I felt the truck fall off the side of the road," the friend reported. "I then realized the truck was going over and down the side of the mountains. Immediately, I looked at my watch and noticed it was 3:00 A.M. There was an awareness we would die at the bottom of the mountainside."

"However," he continued, "in an instant the truck was placed back on the road and everything was fine. I was amazed at how our lives were spared. There is no way to explain how one minute we were in a nosedive going over the edge of a mountain and the next minute the truck was on the road again!"

THE FAITHFUL SHEPHERD

There is no explanation but the faithfulness of God who answers prayer. And what an answer indeed! An incredible intervention by the Lord. But not every story has such a good ending. Why is that so? I have thought about this situation so often as I have looked for answers.

- Was it just a coincidence Brenda woke up and prayed at exactly 3:00 A.M.?
- What explanation can there be for a truck going down the side of a mountain and suddenly being positioned back on the road?
- Are all casualties in life necessary? Can some of them be prevented? How?
- How did Brenda know how to pray?
- Can all intercessors be involved in this type of praying or is it only for special ones?

Since that time, the Lord has helped me discover answers to many of these questions. I now realize we are the Lord's sheep, and *all* His sheep have the potential ability to hear the Lord.

Sometimes we call this type of praying *prophetic intercession*. *Prophecy* or *prophesy* is the Greek word *propheteia*, which means "the speaking forth of the mind and counsel of God."[1] The Greek word for *intercession* is *enteuxis*. Enteuxis means "to meet with, in order to converse." Enteuxis is a technical term for approaching a king and also for approaching God in intercession. In 1 Timothy 2:1 the word means to seek the presence and hearing of God on behalf of others.[2] According to Vine's definitions, intercession is one of the most unselfish things we can do. We are not praying for ourselves but for others. Putting the two words together, *prophetic intercession* means:

· Seeking God's presence in order to converse;
· Meeting with God and hearing Him on behalf of others;
· As a result of seeking, meeting with and hearing God;
· Then, speaking forth the mind and counsel of God.

THE LESSON OF THE CRUNCH

Years ago, I went to a shopping center to pick up decorations for a holiday event. After backing out of my parking space, while I was turning the steering wheel, I heard a crunching sound and felt a bump. Although I had never before been in a car accident, I knew someone had backed into my car.

After getting out and investigating the damage, it was evident what had happened. I was driving a small car at the time, and the other driver did not see me when she started backing her car out of her space.

Dale's response to the incident when I arrived home was, "I should have prayed. This morning as I was driving our car home I saw a vision of the car in an accident. At the time, I did not understand what I was supposed to do and so I did nothing. I thought maybe it was just fear I was experiencing. Now I realize the Lord was showing the accident to me so I could pray that it would not happen."

Needless to say, we both learned a valuable lesson that day. We were new in our spirit-filled walk and did not understand how the Lord speaks to us so we know how to pray. We were thankful for the understanding God gave concerning prophetic intercession. We didn't have a name for that type of praying in those days. We simply understood that God speaks to his people ahead of time and shows us things to come. The cost of the accident was minimal compared to the riches we gained in our knowledge of intercession.

HEARING HIS COUNSEL

In prophetic intercession, we come into the presence of the Lord and hear His mind and counsel. We are then able to pray things that are on His heart. Too often we pray the things that are on our hearts and fail to hear Him. It is through seeking, hearing and speaking forth His mind that we see powerful breakthroughs occur.

As you and I engage in prophetic intercession, we are participating in God's plan for humanity. We are then occupied in having dominion and ruling in the earth (see Gen. 1:26-28). The Psalmist reminds us of this awesome task:

> What is man, that Thou dost take thought of him? And the son of man, that Thou dost care for him? Yet Thou hast made him a little lower than God, And dost crown him with glory and majesty! Thou dost make him to rule over the works of Thy hands; Thou hast put all things under his feet (Ps. 8:4-6).

God made man as His representative on the earth. He sent Jesus to pay the price with His blood and redeem everything man had given away. Jesus then gave authority to His followers to begin to walk in God's plan. His amazing plan includes using us—frail, imperfect humans who have been born again and have His Spirit living within us—to rule over the works of the Lord's hands and to help in the process of putting all things under His feet. Although the completion of that plan is future (see Heb. 2:8,9), God has given us the privilege of participating in that plan now, doing what Adam and Eve were supposed to do in the garden:

> Then the LORD God took the man and put him into the garden of Eden to cultivate it and keep it (Gen. 2:15).

OUR RESPONSIBILITY

God's plan for man involved responsibility. He planned for man to work. The work before the fall was not a form of punishment but one of fulfillment. Work only became drudgery after the Fall (see Gen. 3:15-17). God knew man could not be happy if he were idle. How many times have you heard someone say, "I am so bored"? That statement is usually made with a connotation of dissatisfaction. Knowing man could not be happy if he were idle, God gave man work to do in the earth. The garden did not need to be weeded but did need to be tended. Thorns and thistles were not yet a nuisance. The garden needed to be dressed and kept. Man, as God's steward over the garden, had two responsibilities:

CULTIVATION

The first responsibility of man was to cultivate the garden. *Abad* is the Hebrew word for cultivate. *Abad* or cultivate means to serve; to plow; to worship; to cause to worship.

Zodhiates describes "cultivate" as a priestly role. "In a specialized sense, *abad* means to serve Jehovah in a levitical context."[3] Hosea 10:11 says, "Judah will plow." What does this have to do with us as intercessors? To cultivate is to plow up the ground. Intercession plows up the soil of hearts and causes them to be open to acknowledge and worship God.

Many times people ask me, "Barbara, what kind of ministry do you have?" I usually tell them, "I just plow up hard ground." When I first began answering this way, I did not understand that I was being scriptural. It was the only picture I could give in response to the question.

A few years ago, Dale and I, along with another couple, attended a meeting one night at Christian International in Florida. At the end of the meeting, we were asked to come into

Bishop Hamon's office. After showing us around, he pulled out a tape recorder and prophesied these words to us:

> For the Lord says, "Daughter, when you first hit on two cylinders and two plugs were sparking, you said, 'God, this is great. This is wonderful!' Then it went to four. Then it went to six. You said, 'Oh, my God. What am I going to do with this?' Then it went to eight and you said, 'God, I don't know whether I can handle this or not.'
>
> "But get ready," says the Lord. "You are going to get accustomed to that, and then I'm going to take you to a great big Caterpillar level. And you are going to have great big pistons. You are going to have batteries all over the place charging you up."

When Bishop Hamon prophesied this, I thought, *He thinks I'm a worm, a caterpillar.* Then, I realized he was saying what I say about myself: I am a Caterpillar—a plow! Caterpillar is the brand name for large earthmoving equipment—big plows. You and I, as intercessors, are to plow up the soil of hearts. Cultivated hearts can then be open to acknowledge and worship God.

KEEPING

The next responsibility in the garden was to keep it. The Hebrew word for keep is *shamar*. Zodhiates defines *shamar* as to restrain; to keep within bounds; to hedge around something as with thorns; to watch as a watchman of sheep or cattle; to guard as a prophet.[4]

Adam especially had a responsibility to recognize the pre-existing boundaries of the garden (see Gen. 2:15). He was then to guard the boundaries of the garden in the same way a watchman watches over sheep or cattle. Anything contrary to the Lord's will was not to be allowed in the garden. In other words, he was to exercise great care over the garden as a watchman.

Watchmen in the Bible were to be alert for hostile action against the city. They were to give word to the king of any person approaching the city wall. Another function of the watchmen was to guard the fields and vineyards, especially during harvest seasons. In this definition we see our assignment as intercessors to guard the places assigned to us by the Lord. These places may include our families, our neighborhoods or nations. As we intercede, our prayers will hedge around these places as with thorns, forbidding the enemy's plans.

THE OFFICE OF PROPHET RESTORED

Not all intercessors are prophets, but all can receive a prophetic anointing. The office of prophet has been established once again in the Church during the last decade.

> NOT ALL INTERCESSORS ARE
> PROPHETS, BUT ALL CAN RECEIVE A
> PROPHETIC ANOINTING.

There was a time when the Church did not understand or accept those who stood in the office of the prophet. As the Lord has brought forth revelation, prophets are better received than they were a few years ago. Many did not want to be around those who were called prophets. Some thought they were just wild, ranting madmen. Many times a prophet was pictured as a person who wore weird clothes, ate bugs and had a grudge on his shoulders—shades of John the Baptist. And the enemy effectively used that picture to keep the Church away from the prophets God had sent.

Today, however, there is a general acceptance of Jesus' ascension gift to the Church of the office of prophet. The prophet speaks forth the mind, will and counsel of the Lord. All can receive of the prophetic anointing, since all of us have the potential to prophesy (see 1 Cor. 14:31). The prophetic anointing equips us to speak the mind, will and purpose of the Lord as His voice in the earth.

Julie is an intercessor who often hears from the Lord. During intercession she speaks forth His mind, will and purposes into situations. One night Julie's husband was driving a truck in Arkansas. While asleep at home in Texas that night, Julie dreamed that her husband had fallen asleep at the wheel of his truck. She awoke screaming his name.

Julie's husband had indeed fallen asleep while driving. Suddenly, he heard his wife screaming his name and woke up. Does it seem strange for Julie's voice to reach her sleeping husband's ears at such a long distance? Such powerful intervention by the Lord may seem strange to some but not to Julie. She merely obeys the prompting of the Lord, and He performs the miracle.

In times of crisis when the Holy Spirit alerts intercessors, such questions as these often fill their minds:

· *Is this just fear that I am experiencing?*
· *Do I not trust the Lord to take care of this person or situation?*
· *Am I a person of unbelief rather than faith toward God?*

Many times when the Lord calls us to pray, our mind and the enemy try to talk us out of interceding. We start to question the leading of the Holy Spirit. If we are not alert in the spirit, we can miss what God has called us to do. Julie was alert in the spirit.

In the beginning, God's voice created the earth and all that was made. John the Baptist came later declaring, "I am a voice of one crying in the wilderness" (John 1:23). As a prophetic generation of intercessors, like John the Baptist, you and I are to be *a voice* of the Lord in the earth. The Lord is issuing a call for us to come into His Presence in the "council room" of the Lord and hear what He says. We will always be below God in the hierarchy of the council, but we are still members who have access.

> After these things I looked, and behold, a door standing open in heaven, and the first voice which I had heard, like the sound of a trumpet speaking with me, said, "Come up here, and I will show you what must take place after these things" (Rev. 4:1).

REMOVED, THEN RESTORED TO THE COUNCIL

I believe that God planned for Adam to mature and be part of this Council. But due to his rebellion and fall, Adam was cut off from his destiny. Today, prophets and prophetic intercessors are called to be members of God's Divine Council. They are to stand in the Council of the Godhead, or Trinity. This Council originally included three persons: Father, Son and Holy Spirit. Angels were also a part of this Council (see Job 1:6-12; 2:1-6; Ps. 82:1; 89:7). Several people in the Old Testament were temporary members of God's Council. James Jordan describes some of these incidents in his book *Through New Eyes*:

> Certain Old Testament saints stand as striking examples of Council members/prophets. One is Abraham. When God was about to destroy Sodom, He asked Himself, "Shall I hide from Abraham what I am about to do?" (Gen. 18:17).
> God proceeded to tell Abraham His plans, and asked Abraham what he thought. The remainder of the story is

familiar to everyone. Abraham gave his advice and counsel to God, though always in a deferential manner, respecting the hierarchy. It is in the light of this that we can understand Genesis 20:7, where God told Abimelech regarding Abraham: "Now therefore, restore the man's wife, for he is a prophet, and he will pray for you, and you will live." As a Divine Council member, Abraham the prophet could bring petitions before the Council.

The second great example is Moses, who is the exemplary prophet of the Old Covenant (see Num. 12:6-8), and he is the greatest prophet before John the Forerunner. Moses not only received information from the Council and passed its decisions onto the people, as he ascended and descended Mount Sinai, he also actively argued before the Council when he felt it necessary, even "changing God's mind" on occasion (see Exod. 32:7-14, 30-35; Num. 14:13-19).[5]

Moses was not satisfied being the only prophet. He expressed his heart for God to multiply that anointing to many when he said, "Would that all the LORD'S people were prophets, that the LORD would put His Spirit upon them!" (Num. 11:29). He was really saying, "Oh, that all God's people would be prophets and be able to stand in the Council of the Godhead (Trinity). Oh, that all God's people would hear the sound of the trumpet speaking 'come up here' and hear the conversation of the Godhead" (see Rev. 4:1).

God wanted man to manage the earth as His representative. First of all, man would function in a priestly role. He would cultivate the garden by causing everything around him to want to worship his God. Second, the Lord's plan involved the kingly role of man. He was to *keep* the garden. Man was to carefully watch over the garden to keep away intruders who would violate the Lord's will. Finally, God's plan for man was for him to be a prophetic voice. Man would stand in the presence of the Lord and reason with the Lord as an intercessor. He would then, as God's voice in the earth, speak forth the decisions of the Council of the Godhead.

God has always wanted a kingdom of kings, priests and prophets. As New Covenant people, we are that generation. May we be a people who are like David. Acts 13:36 says David was a man who "served the purpose of God in his own generation." Oh, that history would record that for this generation!

QUESTIONS FOR CONSIDERATION:

1. Have you ever been alerted by the Holy Spirit to pray for someone in a time of crisis when you were not aware of the circumstances?
2. Describe the way you received the call to prayer.
3. How are you cultivating the "garden" the Lord has placed you in?
4. Describe some of the boundaries the Lord has assigned you to "keep." How are you doing it?
5. What do you believe is the "council room" of the Lord?
6. Have you ever been there? What did you do?
7. Describe the connection between prophets, the prophetic anointing and intercession.
8. In your own words, give a definition of prophetic intercession.
9. Who can be used by the Lord as a prophetic intercessor? Are you included?

Chapter Seven

PROPHETIC PROCLAMATIONS

What I tell you in the darkness, speak in the light; and what you hear
whispered in your ear, proclaim upon the housetops.

MATTHEW 10:27

"Please pray for my daughter," the mother cried. "We taught her the Word of God. Jane knows the right thing to do, and yet she has walked away from it. She is now living with her boyfriend, and we haven't heard from her in months."

Jane's mother was obviously in pain concerning her daughter. She had prayed constantly during this ordeal, but there seemed to be no answer to her prayers. Now the request for additional prayer was desperate. Surely, God would hear and answer!

"Heavenly Father," I began. "You are a father and understand the agony of this mother's heart. I ask you in the name of Jesus to bring healing and restoration to this family. Remind this daughter of Your Word. Help her to remember Your goodness." Immediately, I sensed the Spirit of the Lord rise up inside me, along with my faith. Knowing the authority Jesus has given us, I spoke into the atmosphere as if Jane were standing in front of me.

"Jane," I called. "Open your eyes and look. You are in a pigpen. Get up and get out of the pigpen. Come back to your father's house. Come home in Jesus' name!"

A month later I was speaking in a conference at a Bible school. On the way into the auditorium one morning, Jane's mother saw me and came running.

"Barbara," she called out. "You prayed for my daughter, and I have to tell you what happened. When I came home from the conference last month, I found I had received a phone call from our daughter. The time of the call was exactly when you and I were praying. Jane left a message that she was coming home. She said, 'I don't know what happened to me! It was if my eyes were opened and I could see. And I thought, *This is a pigpen. I'm going home.*'"

Late that night after the conference session, several people and I went to a restaurant. As soon as we walked into the restaurant, Jane's mother saw me and came running over. "My daughter is here," she said, as her daughter walked up and joined her, "and she wants to talk to you."

How was this possible? Dallas has thousands of restaurants and yet we were at the same one at the same time. God has an awesome way of orchestrating our steps.

"Thank you, thank you, Barbara, for praying," Jane said, as tears flowed down her cheeks. "Suddenly my eyes opened and I could see the truth." Jane acknowledged her blindness in the situation. However, I wanted answers to some of my questions:

- What *had* happened to bring about such a change in Jane?
- What was different about this prayer from previous times of prayer?
- What had caused the blindness?
- Isn't this type of prayer dangerous for those who are praying?

THE RIGHT PRAYER AT THE RIGHT TIME

Through the study of God's Word, I found some answers. As God's representative in the earth, He has given us the authority to speak for Him. When we speak under the leading of the Holy Spirit, we speak as His voice on the earth. During strategic times, the Lord will prompt us to pray prayers that will bring a breakthrough.

The Bible speaks frequently about the word "time." I like the way Dutch Sheets describes this word:

> The Bible speaks of well-timed (*kairos*) temptations (see Luke 4:13; 8:13). No doubt coincidental temptations occur—a person just happening to be in the wrong place at the wrong time—but there are also well-planned, well-timed temptations. It pays to be alert, both for ourselves and for others. I've had the Holy Spirit prompt me to pray for individuals, especially young believers, with the thought, "It's a *kairos* time of temptation for them." This is what took place in Luke 22:31,32 when Jesus interceded for Peter, praying that his faith not fail him after he denied Christ. It worked.[1]

The word *eth* in Hebrew is the same word as *kairos* in the Greek. Ecclesiastes tells us that there is an *eth* time for every occurrence in the earth. *Eth* means God has orchestrated a strategic time for prayers to break through. By the power of the Holy Spirit, He will alert intercessors to pray during those times. Praying the right kind of prayer at the right time is vital. Since every believer can hear the voice of the Lord, every believer can pray by the moving of the Holy Spirit.

Powerful things will happen as we participate with the Lord at these specific times. God has put the Church on the earth to finish the work of putting Satan under His feet. Ephesians speaks of the work and power made available to the Church:

> In order that the manifold wisdom of God might now be made known through the church to the rulers and the

authorities in the heavenly *places*. . . . Now to Him who is able to do exceeding abundantly beyond all that we ask or think, according to the power that works within us (Eph. 3:10,20).

STRATEGIC DECLARATIONS

According to Ephesians, God is going to make known His wisdom through the Church. The word "known" comes from the Greek verb *gnoridzo*. It is a word that means "to certify, to declare, make known, give to understand, to come to know, discover."[2] To "make known" means that God is going to use the Church to make declarations to the demonic rulers and authorities.

Making declarations to demonic rulers and authorities is really making prophetic proclamations. The Hebrew word for proclaim is the word *qara*. *Qara* means "to call out to, call forth, cry unto, invite or preach. It is usually addressed to a specific recipient and intended to elicit a specific response. Rarely does it refer to a random outcry."[3]

The Greek language has several words for "proclaim." One of them is *katagello,* which means "to tell, to declare plainly, openly, or aloud."[4] *Katagello* has the sense of an offer of information or encouragement. We find this word used to describe one of the results of the communion table:

> For as often as you eat this bread and drink the cup, you proclaim the Lord's death until He comes (1 Cor. 11:26).

When we "take communion," or partake of the elements at the communion table, we are making an announcement or giving a report about the Lord's death.

Another Greek word for proclaim is *kerusso,* a much stronger word. *Kerusso* means "to be a herald."[5] A herald was a public crier who was a speaker of divine truth. The message delivered by the crier was a public and authoritative announcement that demanded compliance. When you *kerusso*, you are like a town crier making a public announcement. This announcement carries with it a level of authority. The authority of the announcement demands that the hearers comply with the proclamation. How powerful!

TOWN CRIERS

We do not have town criers in our cities today. We have newspapers, TV and E-mail to give us information. But, remember the story of Paul Revere? On April 18, 1775 he rode from Boston to Lexington to warn the colonists that British troops were coming.[6] Paul Revere was like a town crier. His announcement of the troops coming to their town carried an authority and the citizens complied by making preparations.

ATTENDANTS AND FRIENDS

Greek literature gives a picture of a public crier. First of all, a public crier was the attendant of a prince, one who performed duties for that prince. He was, however, not just an ordinary attendant. Raised above the status of other attendants, the crier was given a respect and status similar to a friend. As believers, we serve the Prince of Peace. Prince Jesus has raised us to a status like that of the town crier—we are His friends.

> No longer do I call you slaves, for the slave does not know what his master is doing; but I have called you friends, for all things that I have heard from My Father I have made known to you (John 15:15).

Jesus says you and I, as His people, are not slaves but friends. He also says that He will make known to us everything He has heard from the Father. The Greek word meaning "make known" is the same word used in Ephesians 3:10. What does that mean to us as intercessors?

Jesus is going to make known to us the things He has heard from the Father. Intercessors then make known to the evil powers through prophetic proclamations the information received from Jesus. We are not just giving a random outcry, but we are participating in a process released from heaven.

- God the Father makes known (*gnoridzo*) His intentions to Jesus.
- Jesus makes known (*gnoridzo*) the Father's intentions to the Church.
- The Church makes known (*gnoridzo*) the intentions of God to the evil powers through proclamation (*kerusso*).
- The result? Breakthrough!

DEPUTIES OF THE PRINCE

In addition to being an attendant and friend to the prince, a town crier was given a herald's staff. The scepter in the hands of the crier made it clear that as he carried out his commission, he did so under the prince's authorization. In other words, the prince gave him authority to carry out his task.

The LORD says to my Lord: "Sit at My right hand, Until I make Thine enemies a footstool for Thy feet." The LORD will stretch forth Thy strong scepter from Zion, saying, "Rule in the midst of Thine enemies" (Ps. 110:1,2).

When Jesus rose victorious from the grave, He took back the authority man had given away in the garden. Jesus then turned and gave the authority He purchased to those who would follow Him.

> I will give you the keys of the kingdom of heaven; and whatever you shall bind on earth shall be bound in heaven, and whatever you shall loose on earth shall be loosed in heaven (Matt. 16:19).

Proclamation carries with it a nature of binding, commanding and settling. The word "bind" means "to fasten or to tie up with chains or a cord."[7] Prophetic proclamations released through the mouths of intercessors have the ability to tie up the effect of evil powers like an animal tied with chains or a cord.

The verb "loose" means "to loosen, break up, destroy, dissolve, unloose, melt or put off."[8] It is a word that means a reduction to the constituent particles.

When I took chemistry classes we had to memorize formulas. I never did like chemistry and only took the classes because they were required for a degree in nursing. One formula I remember is the one for water: H_2O, two parts hydrogen and one part oxygen.

The uses for water are innumerable. Without it, you couldn't live very long. However, if you were to break up or loose the hydrogen from the oxygen, there would be no water. It would be a reduction of the constituent particles. No longer could the elements do what they were intended to do. When you loose the powers of darkness from a situation, a person or a city, you have done to the enemy what the scientist does to water when he breaks apart the hydrogen and oxygen. Water then is no longer effective to do what it was intended to do. Likewise, through the power of loosing in intercession, the enemy is no longer able to do what he intended to do. The Lord has given us the authority to rule in the earth. Adam had the opportunity, but he gave it away. Because of what Jesus did, once again the Church has been given authority for rulership in the earth.

PROTECTED HERALDS

There is a third picture of a public crier. The Greeks believed that a herald who came in wartime must not be touched. If he were, the one who touched him would incur the wrath of the one who sent the crier and of his gods. The security of the intercessor is his faith

> RULING IN THE EARTH
> IS OUR MANDATE.
> WE DARE DO NO LESS!

in the powerful blood of Jesus. Intercessors are on assignment in a spiritual war. They have been sent by the Captain of the Hosts to do His bidding. A scepter or rod of authority has been given to them. The precious blood of Jesus is the protective covering. Paul said that he "put no confidence in the flesh" (Phil. 3:3). Neither should we. Our confidence is in the power of the blood of Jesus. The Lord has also provided spiritual armor as listed in Ephesians 6. Therefore, ruling in the earth is our mandate. We dare do no less!

CRIER CHARACTERISTICS

Along with the picture of a public crier, there are some general characteristics that apply to all public criers.

UNDER AUTHORITY

The first characteristic is that a crier was always under the authority of someone else. The crier was only the spokesman.

Under the authority of the Lord, we become His spokesmen. Intercessors should always be under authority. A submissive spirit is vital.

Not only are we to submit to the Lord (see Jas. 4:7), but we also need to submit to others on earth (see 1 Pet. 5:5). No person is above the need for accountability. The Bible records the apostle Paul at various times returning to his home church and reporting what happened on his journeys. He was accountable. Throughout the years, I have found great freedom through accountability. I have a relationship with several strong men and women of God who have the freedom to speak into my life. They can see things I cannot see. Each of us has blind spots. We need those who love us enough to tell us the truth. If Paul needed to be accountable, how much more do we in the day in which we live?

THE MASTER'S MESSENGERS

Another characteristic of the crier was that he conveyed the message and intention of the master. He was not to deliver his own message. The central idea was to be able to communicate what the master wanted to be understood. He could not compromise with the one who was receiving the message. He simply delivered the message he was sent to speak.

Have you ever had the enemy try to get you to negotiate compromise? Did he say things like this?

- "Why don't you just quit?"
- "If you don't stop this 'spiritual warfare' praying, you are going to get into trouble."
- "What if your family gets sick or someone you love dies because of this?"
- "Life would be easier for you if you would just be a 'normal' Christian."

Sound familiar? Often, I find people who at one time were very active in their churches, powerful in prayer and helping others grow in their walk with the Lord. As difficulties came into their lives, they settled into a more comfortable place and stopped involving themselves with the Body of Christ or in intercession.

Nancy was one of these people. For many years Nancy taught a ladies' Bible study at her church. She was a vital part of the city-wide intercessory prayer group. Pastors in the city started meeting together to pray. Several times each year churches came together for a time of celebration in praise and worship. Then life started going sour for Nancy.

Finances were tight when Nancy's husband was out of work for six months. Shortly after the layoff, Nancy received news that her son had been caught taking drugs. The pressure seemed too much.

Looking for relief, Nancy decided to stop teaching the Bible study and withdraw from the intercessory prayer group. *Maybe the enemy will leave me alone if I leave him alone*, she thought. Thoughts of quitting bombarded her mind.

After sharing her concerns and thoughts with her pastor, he helped her recognize the enemy's tactics. The enemy was trying to get her to compromise God's will for her life. To withdraw from the Bible study and prayer groups would be to withdraw from those who would help strengthen her.

Nancy made a good decision after she and her pastor prayed. "I will not compromise by backing off," she told her pastor. Months later, Nancy reflected on the Lord's faithfulness in her life. Amazing financial provision came in for her family until her husband was able to return to work. Their son gave his heart to the Lord. After his restoration, he helped other young people walk free from drugs and alcohol. Nancy received tremendous strength from the intercessors who helped pray for him. How thankful she was for her pastor who gave wise counsel. More than ever Nancy now understands why an intercessor cannot compromise with the enemy during a spiritual battle.

JUDICIAL ANNOUNCER

The next characteristic of the crier was that he announced judicial verdicts. What he announced became valid by the act of proclamation. In the American courtroom, a jury decides the verdict for an accused criminal. The verdict is handed to the judge. When the judge announces the verdict, the verdict becomes valid. Intercessors are judges in training. According to Paul, one day we will judge the world (see 1 Cor. 6:2). In the meantime, since Jesus is the righteous Judge reigning from heaven, He hands the verdict to the intercessor. The intercessor then delivers a prophetic proclamation to the evil powers. The verdict becomes valid through the proclamation spoken by the intercessor.

> What I tell you in the darkness, speak in the light; and what you hear whispered in your ear, proclaim [*kerusso*] upon the housetops (Matt. 10:27).

HAMMERING OUT A PROCLAMATION

My family and I were visiting a church in another state several years ago. The church was involved in a building project. To save money, many of the members were helping with the construction.

Dan had been a member of this church for about 10 years. Although most people would not describe him as a preacher, he had a very strong relationship with the Lord. The relationship had deepened considerably over the previous five years. A few years before, his four-year-old daughter had been diagnosed with an incurable disease. The doctors had given no hope. The church joined together and prayed fervently (see Jas. 5:16). Within a few weeks a miracle happened. The daughter was totally healed. The doctors had to report: "It's a miracle!"

Now, years later, Dan had not forgotten God's faithful healing power for his daughter. Most of the men in the church would only work on the building on the Saturdays scheduled as "work days." When Dan came home from work he would head for the church. Late at night the sound of nails could be heard as they were being hammered into the roof. Dan was making an announcement. He wanted the evil powers to hear his verdict: *Jesus is alive. He is the same yesterday, today and forever. He healed my daughter. He is a healing God.* With every blow of the hammer on the nail, by faith he was releasing a proclamation from the rooftop.

WANDA'S PROCLAMATION

While Dan used instruments to make a proclamation, we usually use words. When the Lord was ready to move our family to Dallas, we put our house up for sale. Houses, however, were not selling very well in the East Texas town where we lived. In fact, some houses were on the market for five years or more.

Dale started working in Dallas and commuting over the weekend. We had prayed and done everything the real estate lady told us to do, but the house had not sold. It had been on the market for about eight months. Wanda, a "spiritual daughter," was living with us at the time. Knowing the power of proclamation, Wanda started walking the boundaries of our yard each day during her prayer time. She prayed like this:

In the name of Jesus, I release the favor of God on this house. I command all blinders to come off the eyes of those people needing this house. Eyes, see this house. House, you are sold in Jesus' name.

A command. A prophetic proclamation. Within a couple of weeks the house was sold to the principal of a Christian school. Coincidence? How about a "God incident"?

> But at the proper time manifested, even His word, in the proclamation with which I was entrusted according to the commandment of God our Savior (Titus 1:3).

Paul wrote that at the proper time (*kairos*), he was entrusted with the proclamation (*kerusso*) from the Lord. When intercessors are given the word to speak at the proper time, there will be great victory. Breakthroughs will occur.

God will provide strength to intercessors so that they can do the will of the Lord.

> But the Lord stood with me, and strengthened me, in order that through me the proclamation might be fully accomplished, and that all the Gentiles might hear; and I was delivered out of the lion's mouth (2 Tim. 4:17).

There is a deliverance for God's people and for cities. Let the Lord strengthen you so that the proclamation of His word can be fully accomplished even as it was with the apostle Paul.

QUESTIONS FOR CONSIDERATION:

1. Describe a time when you experienced this public crier anointing. What were the results?

2. List three characteristics of a crier.
3. How do these characteristics relate to intercessors?
4. Describe in your own words the process of proclamation.

Chapter Eight

PROPHETIC ACTS

*And He said to them, "Because of the littleness of your faith; for
truly I say to you, if you have faith as a mustard seed, you shall say
to this mountain, 'Move from here to there,' and it shall move; and
nothing shall be impossible to you."*

MATTHEW 17:20

On August 16, 1997, Chuck Pierce, director of the World Prayer
Center, and I stood looking at the Arkansas River below and at
the huge "Keeper of the Plains" Indian statue towering above the
river. We had been teaching pastors and intercessors at a regional
conference in Wichita, Kansas. Prior to the conference, the Lord
had spoken to Chuck as well as to me that he wanted to use salt
during the conference. Neither of us knew exactly what the Lord
wanted to do with salt. Many times God speaks and we do not see
the full picture of what He is saying to us. If we will be obedient
to take the first step, He will then reveal the next step.

A "SALT COVENANT CEREMONY"

During the conference, we had spoken on the salt covenant and
had the attendees participate in a "salt covenant ceremony."
During the ceremony, the Lord revealed that polluted water was
flowing through the area, and it needed to be purified. That very
day the front page of the local newspaper carried an article about
the pollution in the Arkansas River. City officials were bringing

in experts to see what could be done to clean up the river. God's timing is awesome! It was only by the Spirit of God that we knew about the pollution of the river, and now the news media was reporting what the Lord had already revealed.

A large jar of polluted water was brought to the conference from the river. We poured the remaining salt into the jar of water to symbolically purify it. The pastors and intercessors were asked to meet us at the river at 3:00 that afternoon. Intercessors stood above the river, facing toward the "Keeper of the Plains," while Chuck, the pastors and I went down to the river.

Each of us poured a portion of the salted water into the river and released prophetic proclamations over the river. Some of the pastors proclaimed things such as:

· "I proclaim the polluted river is now purified."
· "The river of bitterness has now become a river of healing and restoration."
· "The curse is broken and this river has become a river of blessings."
· "The Arkansas River is a river where the streams will make glad the City of God."

Later all of us stood beneath the tall "Keeper of the Plains" statue as I read from Psalm 121:

The LORD is your keeper; The LORD is your shade on your right hand. The sun will not smite you by day, Nor the moon by night. The LORD will protect you from all evil; He will keep your soul. The LORD will guard your going out and your coming in From this time forth and forever (vv. 5-8).

We then prayed to break the power of the false god and proclaimed: "The Lord God is the Keeper of the Plains. We trust in Him."

Several months later I received a follow-up written report from an intercessor in Wichita:

There was a series of "artistic" events (ancient rituals) going on at Wichita State University by some Tibetan Buddhist monks, which would culminate on Saturday afternoon in a work of sand art (a sand mandala), representing 50 deities, being dismantled and dumped in our Arkansas River. This would be done in a "sacred" ceremony in order to "bless" (put a curse on) Wichita. Earl Pickard, leader of the Wichita Prayer Movement, was led to go to the river the day before, on Friday, September 5, 1997, and draw out some water which had already been spiritually "purified" by prophetic acts while Chuck Pierce and Barbara Wentroble were here August 16, 1997 (see 2 Kings 2:19-22).

As we arrived, we were all able to find each other at a circular area surrounded by benches. After Earl's teaching and the reading of God's Holy Word, we gathered around a fairly new piece of art which was shaped like the state of Kansas. It was made of tiles which were painted with a prairie scene, Indians hunting, deer prancing about, wolves and fire in the sky. We proclaimed, "God Almighty, You are the Keeper of these Plains."

After singing and praying and praising, we all laid down as palm branches in a path for the Lord to walk across and come to the confluence of the river He created. We were living sacrifices to redeem the evil and ungodly sacrifices which had taken place at this sight. We welcomed the Creator God and THE True Keeper of the Plains. Earl poured the salted and oiled water back into the river to take back any ground gained by the enemy during the Tibetan monks' ceremony.

Then Earl stepped out onto some rocks and tossed driftwood as far as he could into the current of the river to cause the bitter waters to become sweet. We prayed over the bitterness between Kansas and Colorado. We prayed that God would heal wounds and restore relationships.

Then Earl handed each of us a piece of the bread. We took half of our piece and cast it upon the waters. Then we ate the other half of the bread in remembrance of the body of Christ, which has been broken for us. We proclaimed Wichita as the City of Righteous Faith according to Isaiah 1:26. "So be it done on earth, O Lord, Your will and purpose be done as it is in Heaven, regarding our river and our city!" We placed a total of 12 rocks on the bank as a monument and altar in remembrance of what God had done.[1]

PROPHETIC ACTS

What a strange series of prayer meetings! Reading a story like this might cause you to ask some questions:

- What does a little bit of salt being poured into a river have to do with purification?
- Does anything happen when people lie down on the ground like "palm branches"?
- Will one piece of driftwood thrown into a river cause the waters to become sweet?
- Won't people think you are insane if you go around doing weird things like these?

The answer to the last question is "Probably"—that is, if they do not understand what the Bible teaches about prophetic acts as part of intercession. If we look at the meaning of the words "prophetic acts," we can better understand the implication of the term. Webster defines "prophetic" as "having the powers of a prophet; having the nature of or containing a prophecy; predicts or foreshadows."[2] The word "act" is defined as "a thing done; a deed; an action; a decree."[3]

If we put the two definitions together, the term "prophetic act" means a thing or deed done, having the powers of a prophet; an action or decree that predicts or foreshadows.

There are times when the Spirit of God will nudge you to pray in ways that may be different from your usual manner of praying. He may give you ideas or pictures of how He wants you to pray. Some positions include standing, walking, uplifted hands, eyes lifted upward, kneeling or bowing, as discussed by authors Steve Hawthorne and Graham Kendrick in their book, *Prayerwalking*:

> As you become comfortable with some of the standard physical dimensions of prayer, you will find yourself at ease with the other order of prophetic symbols, the *special prayer actions* that God prompts from time to time. God may use these *prophetic symbols* more than we may ever know. Even if they make little sense to us, obedience to the Spirit is what is required. A little bit of faith goes a long way when reinforced with the total concentration of spirit, mind and body (emphasis added).[4]

There are many examples of prophetic acts in the Bible. One illustration is found in the Book of Joshua:

And you shall march around the city, all the men of war circling the city once. You shall do so for six days. Also seven priests shall carry seven trumpets of rams' horns before the ark; then on the seventh day you shall march around the city seven times, and the priests shall blow the trumpets. And it shall be that when they make a long blast with the ram's horn, and when you hear the sound of the trumpet, all the people shall shout with a great shout; and the wall of the city will fall down flat, and the people will go up every man straight ahead (Josh. 6:3-5).

THE JERICHO LESSON

Many times when we look at the condition of our cities or nation we can begin to feel hopeless. After all, the land is filled with every form of evil. Ungodly people rule in government, children are being abused, divorce is at an all-time high and killing the young and the old has become legal. Then there is the problem with occult activity. Witches and fortunetellers now parade across TV screens masqueraded as the "beautiful people." God's people faced a similar situation with Jericho.

The Canaanites who lived in Jericho were devoted to idolatry. They practiced necromancy (communicating with the dead). The city was filled with witches and charmers. Consulting with familiar spirits was practiced regularly. Does this sound like your city? How about your nation?

In the face of all this evil, God had given orders for Israel to take the city. He had raised up a new generation of people. The old generation throughout the wilderness seemed concerned only with its own needs: What will I eat? Will I have water to drink? Fear filled their lives as they looked at the Promised Land. Yet, a new generation went across the Jordan knowing its destiny was ahead. If the promise of the Lord was to be theirs, then cities had to be taken. The first city to be taken was Jericho.

In Joshua 6:2 the Lord had assured Joshua of victory. He was facing a well-fortified, walled city full of idolatry and occultic power. Joshua's part was not to be stronger than the occultic leaders of the city—his part was to be obedient to the Lord. We have the same responsibility today. The Lord requires obedience many times before we see the manifestation of God's power.

SIGNAL JUBILEE

Israel's weapons were very unusual. Rather than swords, spears or arrows, the weapons were trumpets of rams' horns, called *shofars*. What could a trumpet do? These rams' horns were blown, among other things, to signal the year of Jubilee. The horns were prophetic symbols of what was about to happen. Although Jericho, as its inhabitants knew it, was about to be annihilated, the land where Jericho sat was about to experience Jubilee!

According to the Law of Moses, several things were supposed to take place during Jubilee (see Lev. 25:8-22). First of all, slaves were to be set free. God never intended His people to live in perpetual bondage. A path of freedom was promised to them. The second aspect of Jubilee was that the land was to be restored to the original owner. Since God is the Creator, all the earth belongs to Him. The land that was Jericho was about to be returned to its rightful owner. The third characteristic of Jubilee was that debts were to be canceled. God would bring an end to the past and allow a fresh, new beginning.

The spiritual fulfillment of Jubilee is in Jesus. In Luke 4:18,19, He declared that Jubilee had come. As His representatives on earth, we now participate with Him in bringing to the ends of the earth the manifestation of all that Jubilee was meant to be. Joshua led Israel in obedience to the Word of the Lord:

So the people shouted, and priests blew the trumpets;
and it came about, when the people heard the sound of
the trumpet, that the people shouted with a great shout
and the wall fell down flat, so that the people went up
into the city, every man straight ahead, and they took the
city (Josh. 6:20).

RELEASE REVERENCE AND STRENGTH

God did what He said He would do. Joshua and the people carried
out a prophetic act, and God caused the wall to fall and Israel to
take the city. Can you imagine what the sound of the trumpets
did to the Canaanites? The Lord used them for two purposes.
First, the trumpets struck fear in the hearts of the enemy. They
could hear the sound but did not know how many people were
in Israel's army. They certainly did not know what they were
going to do.

The second thing the trumpets did was to release reverence
and strength in the hearts of God's people. When the trumpets
sounded, it was as if God had risen up and they knew the enemy
would be scattered (see Ps. 68:1).

> PROPHETIC ACTS REQUIRE FAITH
> AND PATIENCE TO SEE THE
> PROMISE OF THE LORD.

Faith must be behind each prophetic act. Otherwise, it
becomes a mere physical action, void of power. Hebrews 11:30
tells us that by faith the walls of Jericho fell. The Bible also tells
us that it is impossible to please God without faith (see Heb.
11:6). Because we know we have been obedient to the Lord, we
have faith for a breakthrough. We are saved by faith, filled with

the Holy Spirit by faith and receive promises from Him by faith. If you struggle with faith, pray and ask the Lord to help your unbelief. All things are possible to him who believes (see Mark 9:23,24). Prophetic acts require faith and patience to see the promise of the Lord.

GIDEON'S MODEL

Another prophetic act is found in the story of Gideon (see Judg. 7:16-22). Thousands upon thousands of Midianites and Amalekites were waiting to come against Gideon and his 300 men (see Judg. 8:10). The Lord told Gideon to go down against the camp, for He had given him the victory. Gideon would use several prophetic acts to gain this victory.

SOUND

First, Gideon used sound. Warfare is usually not silent. Sometimes we like to pray in a manner that is comfortable with our personality or culture. It is easy to picture a person who is loud and outgoing involved in noisy intercession. What about the quiet ones? I have noticed even quiet people can make a loud noise when they get excited.

Valerie, a soft-spoken, gracious young lady, was part of the group gathered at a friend's house. A small bug lighted on her sleeve. Valerie, who does not like *any* bugs, screamed, "Oh!" as she brushed the bug off her arm. Suddenly, she had a reason to make a loud noise. In warfare, sometimes we need to make noise to be effective.

Every man in Gideon's army was to blow his trumpet in the loudest manner he could. The men were also to rattle earthen pitchers at the same time. Therefore, the first part of the prophetic act involved sound or noise.

SIGHT

The second part of the prophetic act was visual. God was going to use something the enemy could see. Torches were to be hidden inside the pitchers. When the pitchers were rattled and broken, light came forth. Light coming into the camp of the enemy was a reminder of God's glory cloud (see 1 Kings 8:10,11).

The glory cloud was not a white, fuzzy, fluffy whiff to make a person feel good. God's glory is wonderful for the righteous, but terror for the enemy. Seeing the glory cloud was like seeing into heaven, or at least seeing a representation of God's heaven in the world. In the Bible the glory cloud consisted of such things as light, clouds, lightning, thunder, blue sky and so on. The enemy does not want to be reminded of heaven. Satan was cast out of heaven and will never be allowed to return. Gideon, by using light, reminded the enemy of God's glory that will fill the earth and remove the darkness. Prophetic acts, then, can be visual.

SHOUT

The third part of Gideon's prophetic act involved the voice. The men were to give a great shout: "The sword of the Lord and of Gideon" (Judg. 7:18-20, *NKJV*). Sometimes people tell me they like to pray silently. Sometimes, I also like to pray silently, but not always. There are times when a loud shout is necessary. The important thing to remember is the same thing Mary told the servants at the wedding in Cana: "Whatever He says to you, do it" (John 2:5).

ELAINE'S RESTORATION

A team accompanied me on my second trip to Russia. We stopped overnight in Helsinki, Finland, to rest and pray. During our time of prayer, the Lord revealed to me that He wanted to complete the restoration in Elaine's life. Much healing and restoration had already occurred, but there was still something more that needed to be done.

"Elaine," I prophesied, "the Lord shows me that when your feet touch Russian soil He is going to complete your healing. You have prayed, been prayed for and done everything you know to do. Now you are going to see the healing completed."

Elaine grew up in America with Russian parents. For her, a stigma was attached to her heritage. For some reason, she was unable to get free of the rejection associated with her family roots. As a powerful minister, she prayed regularly for others and saw the Lord set them free. She wanted the same freedom for herself. We prayed and anointed her feet with oil. Her feet would be used to regain ground for the Lord's purposes.

After we arrived in Russia, Elaine began handing out handkerchiefs sent by her mother to the *babushkas* (grandmothers). Her heart was touched deeply by the love coming from these older Russian women. Elaine had always felt embarrassed by her Russian ancestry. Now all she felt was love.

Later, when we arrived in Moscow, the Lord spoke to Elaine to build a memorial in remembrance of what He had done for her. After gathering several small stones, we spent a few days in the city. One day as we were standing in Red Square, the Lord said to Elaine, "This is where you are to build the memorial."

Our group took the small stones and built a small memorial in the middle of Red Square. After praying and thanking the Lord for His deliverance, a tangible presence of the Lord seemed to cover us. We walked down the street to a gift shop. Hanging on the wall was an oil painting of Red Square. The painting portrayed the exact spot where Elaine had built the memorial. She quickly bought the painting.

Today, each time Elaine looks at the painting in her living room, she is reminded of God's great love and healing for her life. She now takes groups into Russia to assist pastors in strengthening the churches. Without the power of God to break through in her life, she would not have been able to fulfill God's destiny for her in Russia. Several prophetic acts were used to help free this captive.

TEMPLE-TOPPLING FAITH

God will use prophetic acts to free individuals as well as to free cities and people. I minister frequently in Southeast Asia. On one of my trips a young missionary from my church in Dallas met me in Malaysia. William ministers in many of the countries in Asia. He had just returned from one trip and could hardly wait to tell me the story of Anna, an intercessor in Burma.

Anna went to a certain spot to pray each day. At 4:00 A.M. she would get up and head to her place of prayer in her village in Burma. After many years a Buddhist temple was built on the spot where she had always prayed. However, this Buddhist temple could not stop Anna's prayers. She continued to go to the area and pray each day.

One day, the Lord spoke to her to do a prophetic act. Anna did not know what to call it. She just did what she felt the Lord was telling her to do. "Take a small stone and throw it at the temple in the name of Jesus," she heard in her spirit. After finding a small stone, Anna threw it at the temple while shouting, "In the name of Jesus." At 4:00 A.M. there was no one around to see or hear what she did.

However, the temple heard! Immediately, the Buddhist temple came crumbling down. It was not long before the police came to arrest Anna. Everyone knew she came to that spot to pray every day. She had done it for years. She was a prime suspect. The police took her to the local police station to question her.

"What did you do?" they questioned. She told them the truth. "I threw a small stone at the temple in the name of Jesus." The fear of the Lord fell on all the policemen. If her God caused a small stone to make a big temple fall, they didn't want to do anything to incite Him to be angry. They immediately released Anna. She had been obedient to perform a prophetic act because of the prompting of the Holy Spirit. God's power was then released, causing the police officials to see the power of almighty God, the true God!

QUESTIONS FOR CONSIDERATION:

1. Have you ever seen a prophetic act done as part of intercession? How did you feel about it?
2. Does it take a prophet to be effective in prophetic acts? Why?
3. Do you ever pray in a manner different from your personality? How did you pray?
4. What are some ways to build faith for unusual ways of praying?
5. Describe the aspect of Jubilee you need the Lord to release in your life.

Chapter Nine

PROPHETIC MUSIC

Let the high praises of God be in their mouth,
and a two-edged sword in their hand.

PSALM 149:6

The last several months had been among the most difficult seasons of my life. Would I ever preach again? I didn't think so. It was one of those times every minister walks through. Hopelessness and failure seem to cover you like a blanket. Your prayer consists of one word: "Jesus." Over and over you repeat the word without hearing a response. Until . . .

GET UP!

"Barbara," the Lord spoke to my heart. I didn't care what He said as long as I could hear Him speak! The heavens had seemed as brass. I wondered where the Lord was in all this. Now hope started rising within me at the sound of His voice. When He spoke, it was not what I had expected. Rather than a sweet word of comfort, the Lord called me to get up out of the place where I was and be strong again. How we want Him to feel sorry for us and just come to our "pity party." For some reason He has never attended any of my pity parties. He simply tells me the next step I am to take.

"I want you to take back what the enemy has stolen from you," the Lord continued. *What did He mean by that?* I wondered.

Pondering the Lord's command, I realized much had been stolen from me during the present crisis. A list of stolen goods formed in my mind. The list consisted of the following: confidence, zeal, finances, friends, vision.

The present crisis was a fire. God's fire is never a pleasant place to be. He sends the fire to prepare us for our destiny. Destruction is never the plan of God for our lives. His fire comes to refine and release the hidden treasures in His vessels.

Part of the hidden treasure the Lord seemed to want to release at this time in me was the authority to redeem. It took several years before I saw total restoration in my life. However, within a short time there was a gradual understanding of the spiritual battle and the weapons I would use to win the victory.

I puzzled for a period of time over the words the Lord had spoken to my spirit. *Does He really want* me *to take back something from the enemy? Isn't that His job? How can I take back anything from the enemy? Do I put on a policeman's uniform and try to arrest the enemy? Should I obtain some type of search warrant and demand restitution?*

CONFIRMING THE PRESENT STRATEGY

Learning to hear strategy in spiritual warfare requires an open heart. Strategies from past victories do not always work in the present battles. Contrast the victory at Jericho with the defeat at Ai (see Josh. 6—7). Formulas do not work in spiritual battles. Therefore, the Lord desires to burn away anything we depend on rather than His voice of direction.

After hearing the Lord tell me to take back what the enemy had stolen, I then listened for further confirmation and instruction. Several days later I turned on the TV. For me this was something very unusual. I love books, so I spend a lot more time reading than watching TV. When I turned on the TV that day, I heard a preacher say, "The Lord spoke to me three months ago and told me I was to take back what the enemy had stolen from me." Wow! Someone else heard the same thing. Over the next several weeks I heard three more people repeat the same instructions from the Lord.

Now I had my confirmation. Jesus said, "By the mouth of two or three witnesses every fact may be confirmed" (Matt. 18:16). There was at least that number of people saying the same thing. One of the ways I check my spiritual hearing is to listen to other prophetic voices. What are they saying? Are they hearing the same thing I am hearing? God does not speak a revelation to only one person. He wants many people to hear what He is saying. Cults usually start by one person hearing a revelation no one else has heard. Peter warned Christians about having a private interpretation of God's Word (see 2 Pet. 1:20).

Now that I had a confirmation of God's Word to my spirit, I needed to understand how to take back the ground lost to the enemy. Several weeks later, as I ministered in meetings on the West Coast and in Canada, I shared the word of the Lord with those attending. "If you are here tonight and you need to take back something the enemy has stolen from you, come forward and let us pray."

In one of the meetings, Tammy dashed to the front of the room. "I want my husband back," she cried hysterically. Questions flooded my mind: *What happened to her husband? Is he dead?*

FLAPPING FLAGS AT TAMMY'S FEET

Suddenly, I felt an inner prompting to do more than just pray a "normal" prayer. After asking the worship leader to lead us in a new song about trampling the enemy under our feet, we began singing enthusiastically. We waved small red flags around

Tammy's feet. The flags symbolized a prophetic picture of the blood of Jesus destroying the works of the enemy against Tammy and her husband. Faith rose up in us as we sensed the power of the Holy Spirit at work. We continued singing, dancing and waving flags around her feet for about 15 minutes. At that time, there seemed to be a "lifting" in our spirits. At such a moment, there is an assurance that the work has been done in the spirit. The intercessors then wait for the results to be manifested in the natural.

A couple of days later I was speaking at a Bible school in the same city. A lady who had been in the meeting came to me. Excitement and joy seemed to cover her.

"Tammy's husband told her before the meeting that he did not want to be married any longer," the lady told me. "He did not want to be a father and he was leaving. On Sunday morning after Tammy attended the Saturday night meeting, he awoke and told his wife he wanted to go to church with her. Sitting at the back of the church, he listened while the minister preached. At the end of the message, he jumped out of his chair, kicked the chair back and ran to the altar. Falling on his face at the altar, the husband gave his life to Jesus, embraced his wife and prayed for restoration in the marriage."

Tammy took back the husband the enemy had stolen! Singing, music and waving flags had been powerful spiritual tools to defeat the enemy. I now realized there was more to music than I had understood. I was amazed I had not seen it before. Scriptures soon "jumped off the page" where music was used in battles:

And every blow of the rod of punishment, Which the LORD will lay on him, Will be with the music of tambourines and lyres; And in battles, brandishing weapons, He will fight them (Isa. 30:32).

The red flags we used to wave around Tammy's feet were what Scripture calls "brandishing weapons." The Hebrew word for brandishing is *tnuwphah*. It is "brandishing as a threat; moving to and fro, shaking the hand as a gesture of threatening, or waving."[1] Many times flags, banners, tambourines or streamers are used in spiritual battles as brandishing weapons.

SPIRITUAL PREPARATION

Another scripture that came alive to me during this time was the one about King Jehoshaphat. He was facing a real battle. Jehoshaphat was in danger and distress due to the foreign invasion of his kingdom by Moabites, Ammonites and their allies. A report had come to him about a great multitude coming against him. No leader had ever been so prepared for battle as Jehoshaphat. Yet he sought the Lord through fasting, prayer and corporate intercession. Nothing is mentioned about equipment, swords, spears, shields or bows. Only spiritual preparation was made.

While praying, the Spirit of the Lord came upon Jahaziel. Some biblical scholars believe Jahaziel was the inspired descendant of the psalmist Asaph. Musicians and worshipers often receive a prophetic anointing. Jahaziel prophesied to Jehoshaphat and the congregation. Through a prophecy, God's strategy for victory in the battle was revealed:

> And they rose early in the morning and went out to the wilderness of Tekoa; and when they went out, Jehoshaphat stood and said, "Listen to me, O Judah and inhabitants of Jerusalem, put your trust in the LORD your God, and you will be established. Put your trust in His prophets and succeed." And when he had consulted with the people, he appointed those who sang to the

LORD and those who praised Him in holy attire, as they went out before the army and said, "Give thanks to the LORD, for His lovingkindness is everlasting." And when they began singing and praising, the LORD set ambushes against the sons of Ammon, Moab, and Mount Seir, who had come against Judah; so they were routed. For the sons of Ammon and Moab rose up against the inhabitants of Mount Seir destroying them completely, and when they had finished with the inhabitants of Seir, they helped to destroy one another.

When Judah came to the lookout of the wilderness, they looked toward the multitude; and behold, they were corpses lying on the ground, and no one had escaped. And when Jehoshaphat and his people came to take their spoil, they found much among them, including goods, garments, and valuable things which they took for themselves, more than they could carry. And they were three days taking the spoil because there was so much (2 Chron. 20:20-25).

BELIEVE THE WORD

Judah and the inhabitants of Jerusalem were told, first of all, to believe the word of the prophets and they would prosper. The prophetic word is given to God's people for their success. The word, however, will not benefit if it is not embraced in faith.

WORSHIP

Next, singers and musicians were sent before the army. How confusing this singing and music must have been to the enemy! Yet it was God's ammunition. As the people obeyed God, the Lord responded by sending a plot to destroy the enemy. He did not send hail, thunder or swords. There was no human strength or power involved. God simply struck the enemy with confusion. The enemies fell on their friends as if they were the adversaries.

Worship and singing are sometimes weapons of warfare. Singing prophetically to the enemy about God's goodness and the enemy's defeat can bring victory. Moses and the sons of Israel sang at the crossing of the Red Sea. Miriam, the prophetess, and the women joined by playing tambourines and dancing. The song included a prophetic portion about the defeat of the enemy in Canaan:

> The peoples have heard, they tremble; anguish has gripped the inhabitants of Philistia. Then the chiefs of Edom were dismayed; the leaders of Moab, trembling grips them; all the inhabitants of Canaan have melted away. Terror and dread fall upon them; by the greatness of Thine arm they are motionless as stone; until Thy people pass over, O LORD, until the people pass over whom Thou hast purchased (Exod. 15:14-16).

Moses, Miriam and the others were singing about the defeat of the enemies in Canaan. They sang that the Canaanites were gripped with terror and dread and were motionless as stone. Did they really believe what they were singing? Probably not. If so, they did not believe it for very long. For 40 years they wandered in the wilderness, fearing the people of Canaan. Leaders who were sent into the land came back reporting, "They make us look like grasshoppers" (see Num. 13:33). All that time the Canaanites were hiding behind the walls of Jericho in fear and terror of Israel. Why were they filled with dread and terror?

They had heard what happened to Pharaoh's chariots and his army at the Red Sea. How did they hear? The prophetic song released what is often called a "spiritual dynamic" to cause the

Canaanites to hear and melt in discouragement and fear. Many times prophetic songs and music release a power to sustain victory for many years. Forty years after the song, the inhabitants of Canaan were still full of terror and dread of the Israelites. Joshua and the new generation born in the wilderness saw the manifestation of the prophetic song of Moses.

MUSIC CAN BRING BONDAGE
OR IT CAN RELEASE
THE CAPTIVES.

Spies were sent to scout out the land, especially Jericho. They found favor with a woman named Rahab. She hid the spies when the king sent men to capture them. Rahab told of the condition of the Canaanites:

> Now before they lay down, she came up to them on the roof, and said to the men, "I know that the LORD has given you the land, and that the terror of you has fallen on us, and that all the inhabitants of the land have melted away before you. For we have heard how the LORD dried up the water of the Red Sea before you when you came out of Egypt, and what you did to the two kings of the Amorites who were beyond the Jordan, to Sihon and Og, whom you utterly destroyed. And when we heard it, our hearts melted and no courage remained in any man any longer because of you; for the LORD your God, He is God in heaven above and on earth beneath" (Josh. 2:8-11).

Think about it! More than 40 years before, a prophetic song had been sung. Now Rahab is saying exactly the same thing that had been sung to a previous generation. God's power is released through the prophetic song and prophetic music as part of prophetic intercession. Music can bring bondage or it can release the captives.

THE POWER OF MUSIC

As I sat in the restaurant with my friend, I found myself getting more and more agitated. What was wrong? We were having a wonderful conversation, yet something was wrong. I wanted to get up and run out of the restaurant.

Recognizing my distress, Helen stopped in the middle of her story. "Let's go to your house so we can visit a little longer. The music in this place is irritating me." Suddenly, I realized what was wrong. I had tuned out the sound of the music in my ears, but my spirit was still sensing it. The music had produced an agitation and brought me into captivity. I had lost the calm, peaceful feeling I brought with me to the restaurant. Upon leaving, the serenity returned. Certain types of music produce captivity, but prophetic music has an ability to release captives.

David was a warrior musician. He was a skillful player on the harp. An evil spirit would come on King Saul and cause him torment. David was sent to play upon the harp during these times of distress. As a result of the music played, Saul was set free from the evil spirit.

> So it came about whenever the evil spirit from God came to Saul, David would take the harp and play it with his hand; and Saul would be refreshed and be well, and the evil spirit would depart from him (1 Sam. 16:23).

Lamar Boschman comments on this in his book *The Rebirth of Music*:

Note here that it was purely on the presentation of an anointed song by a skillful musician that Saul was delivered from the evil spirit. No doctor treated him. It was not a tranquilizer that subdued the disturbing influence of the evil spirit. It was the delivering power of God that was on the harp David played that set Saul free. David didn't sing a word. The anointing was on the instrument and the music that came forth broke the bands that had King Saul tied to the evil spirit.[2]

Prophetic music does more than merely make us feel good. A spiritual dynamic is released to set captives free. God is raising up prophetic musicians and singers today who are involved in prophetic intercession. There is a blending together of intercession and worship. Pastor David Swan in Malaysia writes:

Jesus is not only the Lamb of God, but also the mighty Lion of Judah. The Lion of Judah has begun to roar against the spiritual forces of darkness. This mighty roar is increasing in volume and power through the great army of spiritual warriors. The roar of praise, worship, and warfare is rising and intensifying throughout the world. It is ascending into the heavenlies. It is beginning to destroy satanic strongholds and cast down evil principalities. The prowess of the Lion of Judah is being revealed through His saints.

The paean and crescendo of praise, worship, intercession and warfare is unstoppable! Praise warriors, worshiping warriors and prayer warriors are being raised by the Spirit of God by the multitudes all over the world. The build-up of this victorious army will continue until a mighty shaking takes place in the heavenlies.[3]

The combination of praise and intercession is a formidable instrument of warfare. Paul and Silas used this prophetic weapon when imprisoned at midnight:

> But about midnight Paul and Silas were praying and singing hymns of praise to God, and the prisoners were listening to them; and suddenly there came a great earthquake, so that the foundations of the prison house were shaken; and immediately all the doors were opened, and everyone's chains were unfastened (Acts 16:25,26).

Can you imagine sitting in prison with blood dripping off your back from being beaten and your feet bound by chains? Paul and Silas were in such a situation. The charge was that Paul and Silas were teaching an illegal religion and disturbing the peace. Cultural and religious prejudice added fuel to the fire. Now they sat in prison. It is one thing when we have done something deserving of punishment. It is quite another matter when we are persecuted and falsely accused. Captivity is involved even when no physical prison exists. Times such as this cause us to engage in spiritual battles. Fleshly weapons will not work; only spiritual weapons will be effective in spiritual battles (see Eph. 6:12).

Paul and Silas had no way of knowing God would send a delivering earthquake, since they had not asked for one. Their only hope for deliverance was an intervention by God. Paul and Silas used a spiritual weapon to break their captivity. Dr. Peter Wagner is a strong believer in the effectiveness of praising God as a spiritual weapon.

> Relatively few believers recognize that praise in itself is one of the most powerful weapons of spiritual warfare we have at our disposition. Scripture says that God

inhabits the praises of His people (see Ps. 22:3). The devil cannot long resist praises to God. In Philippi, the major spiritual battle against Python had been won. The forces of darkness were now harassing Paul and Silas with a caning and imprisonment, but they could not maintain their ground in the face of praise and worship. In this case, without any overt confrontation with the forces of darkness, deliverance came.[4]

A MUSICAL MASSAGE FOR MARGARET'S LEGS

Margaret Moberly is a friend of mine and also a faithful intercessor. Several years ago, after suffering from a stroke on each side of the brain, she was unable to move her legs. Margaret was slowly recovering and believing for restoration. Several couples, including Dale and me, went to the hospital for a visit. While there, we prayed for Margaret. During the time of prayer we started singing to her legs:

These legs are full of the life of God,
Paralysis has no power over them.
Legs, we command you to be free and move,
In the name of Jesus.

We continued singing over Margaret's legs for about 20 minutes. After visiting for a little while longer, we left the hospital.

The next morning I received a phone call. Margaret's legs were moving for the first time since the stroke! Was it possible for a song to cause life to come into legs that would not move? Prophetic music unlocks the miraculous and sets the captive free.

Let the high praises of God be in their mouth, and a two-edged sword in their hand, to execute vengeance on the nations, and punishment on the peoples; to bind their kings with chains, and their nobles with fetters of iron; to execute on them the judgment written; this is an honor for all His godly ones. Praise the LORD! (Ps. 149:6-9).

Verse 1 of that same psalm says, "Sing to the Lord a new song." A new song is a prophetic song. It is through prophetic music, song and brandishing weapons that God's people can bring judgment on the enemy. God delights to come on the side of those who have first come on His side in a prophetic celebration of His victory!

QUESTIONS FOR CONSIDERATION:

1. What are some things you feel the enemy has stolen from you?
2. Describe treasures that have come out of a fire in your life.
3. Are there situations where you have used "brandishing weapons"? What were the results?
4. Do you sing prophetic songs (new songs) in times of difficulty? Why?
5. How do various types of music affect you?
6. Is music part of your intercession?
7. How do you plan to use music in warfare now?

Chapter Ten

DANCING, SHOUTING AND CLAPPING

The LORD his God is with him, and the shout of a king is among them.

NUMBERS 23:21

Margaret Moberly had been hospitalized for several weeks following a stroke. During this time she was seldom conscious. However, she was aware of pain. The muscles in her legs would contract so strongly that it would cause her limbs to thrash around in the bed. In her unconscious state, Margaret would scream with pain during the muscle spasms.

After several weeks with no change in the condition, the doctors made the decision to inject alcohol into the nerves of her spine to relieve her of the pain. There was only one drawback. The medication would permanently paralyze Margaret's legs. Since the doctors did not believe she would live, and if she did she would be a "vegetable," why not go ahead and get Margaret out of her pain?

CAROL'S DANCE AND MARGARET'S MIRACLE

The solution sounded so humane. But in times like this, humane solutions are no substitute for the wisdom of the Lord. Carol Cartwright, a ministerial friend of mine, had been with Margaret throughout the time since the stroke. While praying, the Lord spoke His wisdom and strategy to Carol. Carol is a nurse and understood the permanency of the medical procedure for Margaret's legs. Hundreds of intercessors were praying for healing and restoration at this time. How could Margaret's legs be restored if they were paralyzed by this injection? God can work miracles, but would this procedure hinder His will for Margaret? Carol prayed and asked the Lord to reveal His wisdom for the situation.

"Dance during the time of the procedure," the Lord instructed Carol.

"Lord, you know I'm not a dancer," Carol replied.

"Nevertheless," the Lord continued, "I want you to dance throughout the time Margaret is in the operating room."

Dance she did! As soon as the medical attendants left the room with Margaret, Carol danced—and not just some slow waltz. She danced a warfare dance! Carol danced steps she had never seen performed. There was an awareness of a spiritual battle taking place. Had someone come into the hospital room during this time, they would have thought Carol was some wild, crazy woman who went insane due to the stress over her friend's condition. She didn't care. Her focus had to be on God's protection for Margaret.

"It was the best procedure I have ever done," the doctor reported later. "I watched the solution being injected over the monitor. It was perfect," he said as he beamed a big smile of delight.

How surprised the doctor was to discover later that his "perfect" procedure did not work! Margaret's legs were not paralyzed. In fact, they were thrashing around when she returned from the recovery room. Nothing touched the pain. The pain continued 24 hours a day, seven days a week for seven weeks. What had happened? The only explanation was that God didn't let it work. A prophetic dance was used to destroy the power of the enemy's plans.

The pain stopped instantly exactly seven weeks later. (Seven is the biblical number of perfection and completeness.) The cessation of the pain occurred at the exact day of the week and the exact hour when it had started—and it never returned! Later, Margaret recovered from the coma and left the hospital. Since that time she has trained intercessors, led Bible studies, preached and written a book. What a mighty God we serve! The Lord continues to use Margaret to change lives and advance God's kingdom. Could she have accomplished all this in a state of paralysis? Maybe. Maybe not. The Lord must have known what was needed when He spoke to Carol to dance a warfare dance. Sometimes the Lord asks us to do things we are not accustomed to. We may not have great ability or gifting. Our response need only be one of obedience. He gives the power and He gets the glory!

George Otis, Jr. has studied many cultures along with their cultural practices. He describes various occultic practices involving forms of dance in his book, *The Twilight Labyrinth*. James M. Freeman, author of *Manners and Customs of the Bible*, also wrote about this ancient power and practice of dance:

> Dancing was performed at first on sacred occasions only. It was part of the religious ceremonies of the Egyptians as well as of the Hebrews, and was engaged in by many idolatrous nations, and often accompanied with scenes of debauchery.[1]

CANCEL THE COUNTERFEIT, BUT HONOR THE ORIGINAL

Even so, dance is a scriptural aspect of prophetic intercession. God uses our feet to trample the enemy. He also uses dance to rejoice ahead of time in the Lord's victory. God is the One who created dance. The enemy has perverted what God originated. God created dance for His purposes. Believers are learning to hold onto all God has made and only throw out what has been tainted by the enemy.

We find this same premise applies to the doctrine of salvation. The Lord designed the plan of salvation. Those who put their faith in the finished work of Jesus receive salvation. His blood was shed for the remission, or forgiveness, of our sin (see Rom 3:21-26). Repentance and faith in the power of the blood of Jesus give us eternal life. Salvation is not the result of good works (see Eph. 2:8,9). Yet there are many religions today teaching good works to obtain eternal life. Do we throw out the truth concerning salvation merely because some teach a false doctrine? No. We continue to teach the truth. We hold fast to that which is good and true (see 1 Thess. 5:21), and we throw away the false.

The same principles apply to dance. Throw away the evil, demonic and perverted dance of the enemy. Hold fast to the good, true and pure dance created by God for His purposes. Throughout the Bible we are told to dance. Dancing can be a form of worship, a time of celebration or a weapon of warfare used in intercession. Ecclesiastes 3:4 says there is a time to mourn and a time to dance.

SPIRITUAL SHOUTS

Another weapon of warfare used in intercession is shouting. On the third day of a large conference where I was speaking, worship and intercession seemed to reach a peak. Faith had grown in the people after hearing teaching from the Word by several powerful ministers. The prophetic music and song brought to the people a strong sense that the Lord was present with us. An atmosphere of victory over the enemy charged the conference center.

Suddenly, a sustained and spontaneous shout came forth from the nearly 2,000 attendees. The shout was not a short one, nor was it low in volume. For 15 minutes the people continued shouting as one long blast of triumph.

Why were nearly 2,000 people shouting in the midst of praise and worship?

What caused them all to shout for so long with no one telling them to shout?

Was all this just a lot of wild emotionalism?

Whatever happened to things being done "decently and in order" (see 1 Cor. 14:40, *NKJV*)?

There are times in intercession when only a shout will suffice. The Lord is not deaf, but neither is the enemy. Volume is not the issue. Being obedient to the leading of the Holy Spirit is. Dutch Sheets speaks of his own experience of shouting in the course of intercession:

> Truly, there is a time for aggressive, violent spiritual warfare in intercession. I realize many would shrink from such extreme action in prayer—running and shouting at the enemy. There is, however, a time for such spiritual intensity. More than once I have found myself shouting at spiritual powers or mountains of adversity in intercession. I'm not spiritually ignorant enough to believe a certain volume level is required to rebuke evil forces, but the Scriptures do allow for it and even suggest that, at times, it unleashes something in the Spirit.[2]

BIBLICAL EXAMPLES

Scripture shows times when people defeated God's enemies through shouting. Other instances in the Word tell of those who give a prophetic shout of victory before they see the breakthrough.

- Just prior to Jesus' defeat of Satan on the cross, Jesus shouted: "And Jesus cried out again with a loud voice, and yielded up His spirit" (Matt. 27:50).
- The book of Psalms exhorts God's people to "shout" to the Lord: "Oh, clap your hands, all you peoples! Shout unto God with the voice of triumph" (Ps. 47:1, *NKJV*).
- Balaam spoke of God's faithfulness to Israel and said, "The Lord his God is with him, and the shout of a king is among them" (Num. 23:21).
- The people shouted and the wall of Jericho fell: "So the people shouted, and priests blew the trumpets; and it came about, when the people heard the sound of the trumpet, that the people shouted with a great shout and the wall fell down flat, so that the people went up into the city, every man straight ahead, and they took the city" (Josh. 6:20).

Shouting is often an act of faith. There may be no evidence of victory at the moment, yet the Lord delights in those who rejoice in the victory ahead of time. Acts of faith release God's power into the situation. He comes as Warrior to defeat the enemy.

THE LORD'S RETURN

Many believers have read about the Lord ultimately returning with a shout (see 1 Thess. 4:16). Must we wait until the end for Him to return? Can't He return in the power of His presence more than one time? As the Bride of Christ cries out, "Come," the Lord Jesus is going to respond by coming alongside us (see Rev. 22:17).

HEROD'S REVERSE EXAMPLE

Several successes in battle are mentioned in the Bible where shouting was used to secure a victory. In the book of Acts, we read of the crowd of people shouting to affirm their trust in Herod as a god. Because he refused to give glory to God rather than himself, an angel of the Lord struck Herod and he died (see Acts 12:22,23). In the same way shouting brought about the demise of an evil ruler, shouting becomes a spiritual sword in the mouths of believers to destroy God's enemies.

GIDEON

Gideon knew about this spiritual sword. His battle strategy included shouting. Before he faced the Midianites, Gideon took his servant and went to the camp of the enemy to hear what was being said about the battle. Upon entering the camp at night, he overheard a man telling a dream. In the dream, the man saw a symbolic picture of Gideon destroying the Midianites. Another man had the interpretation of the dream. "This is nothing less than the sword of Gideon," he said (see Judg. 7:14). When Gideon heard the men telling the dream and its interpretation, he ran back to his camp and prepared for battle.

One of the spiritual weapons to be used by Gideon's army would be shouting. Later, the men entered the battle using spiritual weapons rather than natural weapons.

Gideon and the hundred men with him reached the edge of the camp at the beginning of the middle watch, just after they had changed the guard. They blew their trumpets and broke the jars that were in their hands. The three companies blew the trumpets and smashed the jars. Grasping the torches in their left hands and holding in their right hands the trumpets they were to blow, they shouted, "A sword for the LORD and for Gideon!" While each man held his position around the camp, all the Midianites ran, crying out as they fled (Judg. 7:19-21, *NIV*).

When Gideon's men shouted "A sword for the Lord and for Gideon!" they were fulfilling the prophetic dream of the man in the camp of the enemy. Not physical swords, but spiritual swords were used. The swords were the shouts in their mouths. The sword coming out of the mouth of intercessors routs enemies (see Rev. 19:21). Effective spiritual warfare causes the enemy to run from the situation.

> The wicked flee when no one is pursuing, but the righteous are bold as a lion (Prov. 28:1).

PAUL

Sickness is an enemy that often will flee from the sound of shouting. The apostle Paul shouted at the paralysis in the crippled man:

> And at Lystra there was sitting a certain man, without strength in his feet, lame from his mother's womb, who had never walked. This man was listening to Paul as he spoke, who, when he had fixed his gaze upon him, and had seen that he had faith to be made well, said with a loud voice, "Stand upright on your feet." And he leaped up and began to walk (Acts 14:8-10).

MANDY, COME FORTH!

Several years ago, I was asked to pray for a lady named Mandy who had been serving alongside her husband as an associate pastor. The couple had recently resigned their positions in the church.

At the request of a friend, Mandy came to the meeting where I was speaking.

One look at Mandy and it was obvious she was suffering from depression. The diagnosis was confirmed when she said, "I just want to die. Life seems so hopeless to me." I was aware that people in Mandy's condition are fragile. Emotions are unstable and sensitivity is needed when praying with them.

Knowing this, I sensed an inner prompting by the Holy Spirit to shout to the depression. I then battled with thoughts assailing my mind: *What if I caused her condition to become worse? Would Mandy be able to understand it was the depression and not her I was shouting at? Was this really the Holy Spirit prompting me to do the opposite of what I would normally do? Could it be the voice of the enemy seeking to further traumatize Mandy?*

The story of how Jesus shouted at the dead Lazarus then filled my thoughts. Lazarus had died and was already in the tomb. Jesus prayed a short prayer for the benefit of those standing around:

And when He had said these things, He cried out with a loud voice, "Lazarus, come forth." He who had died came forth, bound hand and foot with wrappings; and his face was wrapped around with a cloth. Jesus said to them, "Unbind him, and let him go" (John 11:43,44).

Mandy seemed to be wrapped in grave clothes. How she needed to be loosed! I stood looking at her, realizing that if Jesus could call Lazarus from the dead—and if I was His voice in the earth—then I could call Mandy from a place of death.

"Mandy, come forth!" I shouted. "Grave clothes, turn her loose in Jesus' name." Mandy slumped to the floor under the power of the Holy Spirit. Later, she told me she felt something unwrap from her when I shouted the command.

The next day Mandy was at the meeting again. No one had to ask her to come this time. She came to me laughing and rejoicing for her breakthrough. The depression she had fought for several months was gone. She woke up that morning singing and dancing. Her family was amazed at the transformation!

Over the next several years when I was speaking at meetings in her area, Mandy would always be there. She never experienced the depression again. Later, she and her husband successfully served in leadership at another church.

ONLY THE HOLY SPIRIT KNOWS WHAT WILL BRING DELIVERANCE AND HEALING TO THE CAPTIVES. SHOUTING IS JUST ONE OF THE TOOLS HE CALLS US TO USE.

Formulas do not work in these situations. Only the Holy Spirit knows what will bring deliverance and healing to the captives. Shouting is just one of the tools the Spirit of God uses in intercession.

CLAPPING

Another tool in prophetic intercession is clapping. There are times in intercession when it seems appropriate to clap. There is a sense of warfare. During many of these times I feel compelled to clap at the enemy. Does this sound strange to you? Have you ever had a pet do something you did not want it to do? After a few times of telling it to stop, did you ever clap your hands at your pet? What happened? Didn't your pet usually stop what it was doing and run from the situation?

There are times in intercession when we deal with the enemy

and his schemes. After a while, something inside us rises up and says, *No!* Clapping our hands at the enemy follows the authority and finality of our decision. The clap seals our decision for him to back away from his maneuvers.

CELEBRATION CLAPPING

Clapping is usually associated with a time of joy and celebration. Clapping can be an expression of approval or rejoicing. Sometimes people applaud presidents, kings and other meritorious individuals by clapping when they enter a room. We are instructed in the Bible to honor the Lord in a similar fashion:

> O clap your hands, all peoples; shout to God with the voice of joy. For the LORD Most High is to be feared, a great King over all the earth (Ps. 47:1,2).

VAMOOSING VARMINTS

There are other times when clapping is not a symbol of rejoicing. A few months ago I was privileged to stay in the home of a lovely couple in the hill country of Texas. Fran invited me to see the garden she and her husband had planted. How wonderful it was to be outside and smell the flowers and freshly mown grass.

As we walked across the lawn and around the side of the house, Fran noticed several "critters" in her garden. "Oh, no!" she exclaimed. "They're back again." I watched while Fran ran toward the garden, quickly clapping her hands toward the four rabbits that were nibbling away at the fresh vegetables. Hopping frantically over the rows of carrots and cabbage, the rabbits disappeared into the woods.

Fran was not expressing a sense of joy or rejoicing through her clapping. On the contrary, she was striking her hands together in anger at the rabbits. They were enemies of her garden. Job speaks of this type of action to be used against the wicked:

> Men will clap their hands at him, and will hiss him from
> his place (Job 27:23).

Ezekiel alluded to this form of abasement in speaking of the destruction of Tyre. Ezekiel 28:14 calls the king of Tyre "the anointed cherub who covers." Many people believe this passage refers to Lucifer before he fell from heaven.

Tyre was an ancient city notorious for wealth and prosperity. The city engaged in idolatry. Pride filled the hearts of the inhabitants. But the destruction of Tyre was sudden:

> The merchants among the peoples hiss at you; you have
> become terrified, and you will be no more (27:36).

Matthew Henry said, "When God casts his judgements on the sinner, men also shall clap their hands at him and shall hiss him out of his place."[3]

CAPHAG

There are a couple of words in Hebrew used to describe clap. One word is *caphag*. *Caphag* means "to show derision or grief or indignation; punishment; to strike, to slap (the thigh, i.e., a cultural sign of indignation or lamentation)."[4]

This word is used in the story of Balak. When Balaam refused to curse the enemies of Balak, Balak became indignant and clapped his hands against Balaam.

> Then Balak's anger burned against Balaam, and he
> struck his hands together; and Balak said to Balaam,
> "I called you to curse my enemies, but behold, you have

persisted in blessing them these three times!" (Num. 24:10).

TAQA

Another word in Hebrew for clap is *taqa*. There are several meanings to this word. Some of the meanings are "to clatter, to slap or clap the hands together in rejoicing or at another's misfortune; to strike or drive (a nail, a tent peg, a dart); to thrust or drive a weapon."[5]

Remember the story of Jael in the book of Judges? The word drove is the Hebrew word *taqa*. Jael drove a weapon (nail) through the head of Sisera.

> But Jael, Heber's wife, took a tent peg and seized a hammer in her hand, and went secretly to him and drove the peg into his temple, and it went through into the ground; for he was sound asleep and exhausted. So he died. And behold, as Barak pursued Sisera, Jael came out to meet him and said to him, "Come, and I will show you the man whom you are seeking." And he entered with her, and behold Sisera was lying dead with the tent peg in his temple.
>
> So God subdued on that day Jabin the king of Canaan before the sons of Israel. And the hand of the sons of Israel pressed heavier and heavier upon Jabin the king of Canaan, until they had destroyed Jabin the king of Canaan (Judg. 4:21-24).

SPIRITUAL TENT PEGS

Israel was completely delivered out of the hand of Jabin king of Canaan. Although the above scripture says "God subdued on that day Jabin," He used a woman to assist Him with the job. God will subdue his enemies through faithful warriors. When these warriors clap their hands against the enemy in intercession, they are doing the same thing Jael did when she drove the tent peg through the head of Sisera. Did you ever think clapping in intercession could be such a powerful weapon?

QUESTIONS FOR CONSIDERATION:

1. Describe your spiritual perspective on dance.
2. Have you ever danced as part of intercession? Why?
3. Describe a time of victory in your life when you shouted. Why did you shout?
4. List several events where you have seen people clap. Why were they clapping?
5. Have there been times when praying that you sensed a prompting to clap your hands? Describe one of those times.
6. Why can't a person just pray and not be "emotional" by dancing, shouting and clapping?

Chapter Eleven

PRAYERWALKING

My people are destroyed for lack of knowledge.

HOSEA 4:6

East Texas. Spring 1976. Fervor and optimism were high. We were the newly elected area board for Women's Aglow. All we knew to do was pray, and pray we did!

After a particular prayer session, an inner prompting in our spirits told us that we should drive to a small town a couple hours away and pray for the town. As we caravanned to the sleepy, quiet town on a Thursday afternoon, we sensed we were being sent on a divine mission.

Alongside a quiet street at the edge of town, we parked the three vehicles and promptly scrambled out the doors. Excitement filled the air. Did the residents of the town know God was about to blow a fresh wind of His Spirit through their area? There was no doubt in *our* minds that it would happen.

As we walked down the streets, we prayed, "Lord, come and visit this town. You created these people for Yourself. Please deliver them from the hopelessness and helplessness that plague them. Raise up a people in this place who will bring glory to Your name. Release revival fires of Your Spirit. Forgive us and these people for lukewarmness and complacency. Bring forth a group of women who will set an example of godliness."

The prayer continued as we walked. The more we prayed, the more our faith grew.

MAPPING THE MARCH AND MARCHING THE MAP

The map! Where was the map? Someone ran to the car. Returning with the prized piece of paper, each was aware of the next step. After locating the town on the map, hands were laid on it as we covered the spot where the town was located. "We declare Jesus is Lord over this place!" we proclaimed.

Dr. Peter Wagner writes about intercessors using maps to assist in times of prayer:

> Prayer has a geographical dimension and therefore many experienced intercessors are interested in maps. The walls of my prayer room are covered with maps. On one wall I have a world map; on the other wall is a huge map of Stockholm. I have been encouraged by some of my friends who also have maps in their prayer rooms. Many times I stand in front of the world map when I am praying.[1]

After folding the map, we returned to our cars. Sensing our mission was accomplished, we drove back home. A feeling of satisfaction filled us knowing we had done what the Father asked us to do. Our eyes didn't see anything change that day. People passing by probably just thought a group of strange women was having fun. However, we had confidence knowing what happened in the Spirit that day would surely be manifest in the natural at a later time.

WITNESS TO THE RESULTS

Several years later I had the privilege of speaking at a Women's Aglow meeting in that town. I'll never forget the joy of walking into the room overflowing with women. What a powerful Presence of

God was in that room. Later during the meeting, many people were saved, baptized in the Holy Spirit, healed and set free. The prophetic word brought encouragement and direction to many who were seeking answers from the Lord. The same fervor experienced on the prayer walk several years prior was in the room that night. At last, after several years of believing in faith, a fresh wind of the Holy Spirit was blowing in this town. "Lord, You really were leading us that day, weren't You?" I gratefully prayed.

I was reminded of Moses and the mission the Lord assigned to him. In Exodus 3 the story is recorded of Moses' commission to deliver the children of Israel out of Egypt. Moses questioned the Lord in choosing him to do such a thing. God assured him that when he brought the Israelites out they would worship the Lord at Mount Horeb, the mountain of God. There would be a manifestation in the natural of what God had spoken. Moses would then know it was the Lord leading him on his mission.

Now as I stood before the room of women, the evidence of God's faithfulness was in front of me. There was a manifestation in the natural of what happened in the Spirit several years before. Walking—and prayerwalking—with the Lord is never dull!

BIBLICAL PRAYERWALKERS

Since those early beginnings of walking and praying, the Lord has continued to bring understanding of the value and scriptural basis for this type of prophetic intercession. I have discovered many people in the Bible who walked cities and regions under the inspiration of the Holy Spirit. Their lives testify of God's intervention to redeem and restore entire cities and regions as a result of their obedience.

ABRAHAM

Abraham was a man in the Bible who was a "prayerwalker." God
wanted to give Abraham a vision of his inheritance. To understand
the magnitude of God's promise, it was necessary for him to
walk and look at the land.

> And the LORD said to Abram, after Lot had separated
> from him, "Now lift up your eyes and look from the
> place where you are, northward and southward and
> eastward and westward; for all the land which you see, I
> will give it to you and to your descendants forever. And I
> will make your descendants as the dust of the earth; so
> that if anyone can number the dust of the earth, then
> your descendants can also be numbered. Arise, walk
> about the land through its length and breadth; for I will
> give it to you" (Gen. 13:14-17).

Abraham was walking a prophetic walk. Although he would
not see the promise of God fulfilled in his generation, his
descendants would inherit the land. As Abraham walked, faith
would arise for him to be able to inherit the promise.

Faith is a key for unlocking breakthroughs in intercession.
Receiving from the Lord requires faith. A person receives salvation
not by good works, but by faith in the finished work of the Cross
(see Eph. 2:8,9). Being filled with the Holy Spirit requires faith (see
Acts 2:38,39). Healing and deliverance are often the result of faith.
It is through faith that we receive the promise. When prayerwalking, it is important to walk and pray faith-filled prayers.

> Now faith is the assurance of things hoped for, the con-
> viction of things not seen. For by it the men of old gained
> approval (Heb. 11:1,2).

As Abraham walked the land in faith, he received vision of the promise for his descendants. Many years would pass before his son Isaac was born, and still many more years before more descendants would be born. Yet, throughout his life, there would be a strong visual impression to remind Abraham of God's promise.

The term "prayerwalking" is merely an expression used to define a particular function in intercession. I like the way authors Steve Hawthorn and Graham Kendrick describe this word:

> Many people have begun to use a new word to describe the recent burst of citywide intercession. Yet to walk while praying is probably not a new activity, though it seems different from the well-known formats of prayer. The rising interest is so substantial that it can only help to add a new word to our vocabulary: *prayerwalking*. We define prayerwalking simply as *praying on-site with insight*.[2]

Today, people all over the world report breakthroughs attributed to prayerwalking. One such report comes from Hong Kong. A team of intercessors walked and prayed around a temple in Hong Kong during the summer of 1997. A leader of the intercession team proclaimed over the area, "Jesus is Lord!" Later it began to rain. In fact it rained so hard the intercessors had to leave. At 5:00 the next morning there were mudslides as a result of the rains. The media reported the results of the mudslides, but most were unaware of the prayer walks just prior to the rain. One magazine gave the following report:

> On July 1 of last year, 40,000 Buddhists gathered in a stadium in Hong Kong to mark the end of British rule of the colony. These people were celebrating the fact that Hong Kong is now officially part of China again.

But one day after the festivities, at 5 A.M. on July 2, disaster struck. Torrential rains triggered mudslides, which severely damaged the Ten Thousand Buddhist Temples in the Shatin sector of the city. Sacred statues were broken into pieces, the foundation of the temple was ruined, and the government has since ordered it closed. The temple housed 13,000 idols, including the largest indoor Buddha statue in Hong Kong. Dennis Balcombe, who has pastored Revival Christian Church in Hong Kong since 1978, believes the disaster was a sign of God's judgment on the ancient Buddhist religion. And he believes the unusual incident signals a new day for China.[3]

JOSHUA

Another man mentioned in the Bible as a prayerwalker was Joshua. He walked the land to gain knowledge of the people as well as the problems of the land. Knowledge is important in prayer. The more we know about a situation, the more accurately we can pray. Armies spend a great deal of time and effort studying the battlefield before engaging in taking over territory.

Sometimes as intercessors we want to jump into a spiritual battle for a people or territory when we know nothing about the situation. One reason for a lack of results in our prayer life can be a lack of knowledge. Our prayers might be sincere, but they might not be as effective as they could be because we don't know how to pray accurately.

Joshua gained knowledge through walking the land. Forty years before crossing the Jordan River to possess the Promised Land of Canaan, Joshua, Caleb and 10 other leaders walked the land. They inspected the land and returned to Moses with a report of their findings. God had made a promise to Abraham more than 400 years before. However, it was not enough just to know that God had made a promise. It was important to gain knowledge of how to receive the promise. Walking the land would help give strategy. The sad part of the story is the fact that, of the 12 spies, only two had faith to believe God's word to them. The report from Joshua and Caleb provided the information needed for a nation to receive their inheritance:

> And Joshua the son of Nun and Caleb the son of Jephunneh, of those who had spied out the land, tore their clothes; and they spoke to all the congregation of the sons of Israel, saying, "The land which we passed through to spy out is an exceedingly good land. If the LORD is pleased with us, then He will bring us into this land, and give it to us—a land which flows with milk and honey. Only do not rebel against the LORD; and do not fear the people of the land, for they shall be our prey. Their protection has been removed from them, and the LORD is with us; do not fear them" (Num. 14:6-9).

Fear is a terrible enemy. It will keep a person from God's best. It is important in intercession to guard against fear. I love the story told about Smith Wigglesworth. He was asleep one night and awakened to see a form at the foot of his bed. After recognizing the form in his room as Satan, his reply was calm and void of fear. "Oh, Satan, it's just you," he said, and immediately rolled over and went back to sleep.

God has promised to give us an inheritance. His power is stronger than the power of the enemy. Remember the faithfulness of God in previous battles. Courage will then replace fear.

> If you should say in your heart, "These nations are greater than I; how can I dispossess them?" you shall not be afraid

of them; you shall well remember what the LORD your God did to Pharaoh and to all Egypt: the great trials which your eyes saw and the signs and the wonders and the mighty hand and the outstretched arm by which the LORD your God brought you out. So shall the LORD your God do to all the peoples of whom you are afraid (Deut. 7:17-19).

Ten of the 12 spies were afraid of the people in Canaan. Joshua and Caleb were of "another spirit" and believed God more than believing the fear-filled facts. As a result of gaining knowledge and walking in courage, they received the promise of the Lord.

Dutch Sheets, in his book *Intercessory Prayer*, tells the story of Sue Doty, who prayerwalked and gained knowledge so she could pray effectively. As a result, there was a powerful breakthrough in her city.

I sensed the Lord wanted me, along with a team of inter-cessors, to go on a prayer walk over a specific route, but that some preparation was necessary. First, I talked with my pastor about this and then went to drive along the route I knew we were to prayerwalk. As I approached a theater (X-rated movie house, video shop and bookstore) the Holy Spirit started to give me specific instructions. He told me to cast out the spirits of pornography and lust, and I did so. He also told me to pray in the Spirit. After a short time I was released from praying, and I con-tinued on the rest of the route before going home.

On that Friday the Lord revealed to me what had actually happened. I turned on the local news to hear that this particular theater had been ordered by the city to close its doors. The day after I had been there to pray, the city conducted a surprise inspection. The theater was cited for several violations and its doors were immediately closed and locked.[4]

NEHEMIAH

Another reason for prayerwalking is to help identify with the people being prayed for. Nehemiah walked Jerusalem not only to gain knowledge but also to help him identify with the people of the land. He was employed as the cupbearer to the king in Susa. Although he lived a distance from Jerusalem, he wept and mourned over the condition of God's people.

AS WE WALK AND PRAY, THE LORD WILL HELP US TO IDENTIFY WITH THE PAIN AND CONDITIONS OF THOSE FOR WHOM WE ARE PRAYING.

After gaining permission from the king, Nehemiah went to Jerusalem. He traveled throughout the city to inspect the broken-down walls and the gates that had been burned. Nehemiah's heart was burdened with a desire to see Jerusalem restored and the reproach removed from the people.

Then I said to them, "You see the bad situation we are in, that Jerusalem is desolate and its gates burned by fire. Come, let us rebuild the wall of Jerusalem that we may no longer be a reproach." And I told them how the hand of my God had been favorable to me, and also about the king's words which he had spoken to me. Then they said, "Let us arise and build." So they put their hands to the good work (Neh. 2:17,18).

As a result of Nehemiah's prayers, his walking the city and his identification with the people of the land, the city was restored and the enemy put to flight. As we walk and pray, the Lord will help us identify with the pain and conditions of the people in an area.

IN THE LAND OF REVELATION'S SEVEN CHURCHES

Many people live their entire lives without the blessings of God. Ignorance and false religions keep them blinded to the love and forgiveness available through Jesus Christ. Believers who walk and pray have opportunities to share God's great love to them.

Mike Haught tells the story of an encounter with Muslims who do not understand the power of forgiveness. He went as part of a prayer team to prayerwalk in Turkey.

Modern Turkey is the "Asia" of the book of Acts. The term "Christian" was first used in Antioch, modern-day Antakya. All seven churches of Revelation are located in Turkey. Many of Paul's writings were addressed to churches found in Turkey. Yet a land with such a heritage from the Lord is today 99 percent Muslim with just a tiny remnant of Christians.

Second Samuel 14:14 says: "Yet God does not take away life, but plans ways so that the banished one may not be cast out from him." God did not take away the life of the gospel in Turkey; the enemy stole it. But God is making a way for those banished ones to return to Him. Mike tells the report about forgiveness in Turkey:

> For the last three years teams of believers have been walking the route of the Crusades from northern Europe to Jerusalem. They are presenting the message of reconciliation to those people groups impacted by the

atrocities committed in the name of Christ. In May of 1998, I was privileged to be on one of those teams. Our target was Turkey. The group walked seven major cities, praying and offering the message of forgiveness and reconciliation.

Our communication was mainly through dictionaries and sign language. However, the message which was printed in both English and Turkish was still understood.

As my son and I were in a marketplace in Adana bargaining for some of those wonderful Turkish towels, my son had a captivated audience of ten or twelve men. He was wearing a T-shirt with the Turkish map and the forgiveness message on the back. As he shared the message verbally through an interpreter, some men behind him, with their fingers on his back, were tracing the Reconciliation Walk path. From where I was standing, I could see most of their faces and the joy that came to them as they received the message. Even with their limited understanding of forgiveness, they were able to receive and understand the apology.

The Turkish people were very hospitable and we were welcomed into shops and homes freely. School children on the streets rallied around us with genuine desire to communicate and learn more from us. We found the hearts of the Turkish people open and eager for the Truth. The most frequent expression we heard was, "This is a good thing you are doing." I know there were seeds planted that will be harvested in the future. God is calling the nations to Himself. He is redeeming what has been taken away in the land of Turkey. The Word of the Lord is being proclaimed throughout that land and the people who were sitting in darkness will see a great light (see Matt. 4:16).[5]

Jasper's Reconciliation

Alice Patterson is another person who prayerwalked a town involved with pain. On Monday, June 8, 1998 CNN news reported the torture and racially motivated murder of James Byrd, Jr., in Jasper, Texas. Alice felt the Lord directing her to go to Jasper and pray.

John, Cathe and I felt that we were to drive to Jasper to attend a rally calling the city to prayer after the murder of James Byrd, Jr. It was to be held at the Town Square in downtown Jasper. Rev. Charles Burchett asked us to go early and prayerwalk the area. As we circled the square first in our vehicle, we secured the perimeter, and asked God to pour out His Spirit. Pastor Mike Sheffield and his wife, Millie, saw us get out of the car with our Pray Texas sign on it, welcomed us and asked us to pray and intercede for the meeting. He said that people in the area did not understand intercession. At the invitation of these local pastors, we went straight to our assignment.

As we began to pray first at the gazebo where the speakers would stand and then on the lawn, we noticed an almost "party" spirit. It was like, "We're going to be on TV!!!" Huge media trucks from the major networks and CNN lined the streets around the courthouse. The world was watching Jasper.

As we walked around, it was beginning to sprinkle and the wind was getting up. As we passed a media truck, the reporter said, "We just got a feed from

Houston. A major storm is heading straight for us with strong winds and pouring rain." Next prayer assignment—pray that the storm will miss us. It did! The wind stopped blowing, the sun came out and a gentle breeze began to blow.

The people settled down and a youth choir made up of mostly black children and a couple of white girls began to sing, "How excellent is Your Name, O Lord, how excellent is Your Name." When they sang, "Amazing Grace," the crowd joined in. Then there was a prayer followed by a chorus, another prayer, another chorus. The people were attentive. It was a nice service, but there had not been a knitting of the hearts of those in attendance. However, the Lord saved the day.

As everyone was dismissed and turned to leave, an older gentleman on the front lawn turned around, put both arms up in the air and shouted, "Everyone, hug somebody!" When he shouted those instructions, something in the atmosphere broke. His shout gave us permission to spread love and reconciliation around. Everyone started laughing, hugging and telling each other, "God bless you. I love you."

As I hugged a black teenager, we embraced and then clasped hands. He looked me square in the eyes and said, "This is going to work. I really believe this will work." God performed a miracle and that little senior citizen had "the word of the Lord" for the moment. And perhaps it's the word of the Lord for every moment, "Everybody, hug somebody."[6]

I agree with Alice. "Everybody, hug somebody" needs to be the word of the Lord for every moment. Somehow, I sense the

Lord will use prayerwalking in more places than Jasper to cause this to happen. God's ways are amazing!

QUESTIONS FOR CONSIDERATION:

1. What is the purpose of maps in intercession?
2. What are some ways to realize the effectiveness of prayerwalking?
3. Why does a person need to see a physical place while he is praying?
4. Describe the necessity of faith in prayer.
5. Can't a person just pray in faith and have God answer his prayer? Why is it necessary to gain knowledge about the situation? After all, God knows everything about the problem.
6. How have you dealt with fear in your life?
7. Have you ever identified with the pain and feelings of others you have prayed for? How did it affect the way you prayed for them?
8. Have you hugged somebody today?

Chapter Twelve

PREVENTING BACKLASH

You may have to fight a battle more than once to win it.

— MARGARET THATCHER

"Barbara, I'm calling from my car. Pam has been in a car accident. There is a traffic jam, and I can't get to her. I'll call you later when I have more information." Bobby Anderson hung up the phone.

THE ENEMY'S ASSAULT

What happened? I stood holding the phone in my hand, stunned from the phone call. Pam was scheduled to pick me up at my house in about 10 minutes. I was to speak at my church for the evening service. Pam had planned to drive me. She had just started working for my ministry two weeks before. Pam not only had a sharp business mind but also was a close friend. How could I speak in half an hour when I didn't know the condition of my dear friend?

"Lord, surround Pam and Bobby with your love and protection," I prayed. "Assign your choice of doctors and medical personnel to Pam. Release your angels to do battle for them. And while you are at it, Lord, I need your grace and peace."

After the evening service, Dale and I drove to the hospital. Bobby was there and gave us a report. Pam was driving to my house when a drunk driver crossed several lanes of traffic on the interstate, crossed the median and then crossed several more lanes of traffic. He hit the back of Pam's van without her ever seeing him. Several people witnessed the accident. Pam's van spun around and then rolled off the freeway. Later, Pam only remembered sensing her van rolling and crying out a one-word prayer, "Jesus!"

Five and one-half hours later the hand surgeon completed his task of connecting severed ligaments and stitching the skin back together. How thankful we were to learn that her face was untouched and the rest of the injuries were only small cuts requiring several stitches and some skin scrapes! However, the van was totaled.

Even though we were grateful to the Lord for his protection in Pam's life, we now had a problem for the ministry. Pam would not be able to do any office work for several months. Her hand would require therapy several times a week. Where would we find a person to take her place?

The following Sunday Marilyn walked over to me at church. "Barbara, I feel the Lord has told me I need to help you with the ministry," she said.

"When can you start?" I asked excitedly. We were already behind in some work and needed instant help.

Two weeks later, after Marilyn began working for the ministry, her husband arrived at the Park-n-Ride lot just in time to see someone driving away with his car. A couple of days later the car was found abandoned in a ditch full of water. The car was beyond repair. Marilyn and Gary now needed another car but were not in a financial condition to buy one.

Several days after that, a couple at the church sold them one of their cars at an affordable price. After driving the newly acquired car home and parking it, they went to the church to attend a memorial service for a young single lady who had been violently murdered. Leaving the church, Marilyn and Gary drove up the ramp to enter the freeway. As they approached the freeway, a woman in a nearby car pulled out a gun and pointed it toward them. How thankful they were that the lady did not pull the trigger! However, they were coming from a memorial service, and this gesture didn't help their emotional state.

Pulling into their parking area at home, the Gibsons discovered that the newly acquired car they parked five hours ago was missing. It had been stolen.

What was going on? Why were these things happening to the people who worked for me?

How could the enemy have access to the lives of these spirit-filled people? Was there an open door allowing the enemy this access? If so, where? And if the door was open, how should we close it?

"Lord," I prayed, "I must have an answer. I will not bring another person into this ministry until I know what to do."

For several days, I pulled aside to fast and pray. I started down my mental checklist of spiritual considerations:

· These people were all walking with the Lord.
· There was no sin we were aware of in their lives.
· Their homes were in order.
· All were serving the Lord in the best way they knew how.

Why then were we facing a pattern of tragedies? Could the difficulties we were encountering be part of the enemy's backlash? We felt it was.

INCREASED MINISTRY REQUIRES INCREASED INTERCESSION

After several days of prayer, the Lord revealed a spiritual principle to me. It is a principle that has changed my personal life and the life of my ministry: With every expansion or increase in the ministry, there must be a corresponding increase in the base of intercession to hold it up.

A simple truth. Why had I not seen it before? And how would I increase the base of intercession? I reflected on the current prayer and intercession taking place in my ministry. Intercession was already a vital part of the ministry. Not only did I teach and demonstrate prayer, I prayed! A typical day for me included several hours in prayer and study of the Bible. About 200 intercessors around the United States prayed for me on a regular basis. Each month I sent a prayer letter to keep them informed of items needing prayer. Several retreats for the intercessors were held to encourage and strengthen them. Now I needed new strategy. Apparently the present base of intercession was not enough to sustain the growing ministry.

A familiar scripture came to mind. It would not leave. Maybe God was trying to say something to me:

How could one chase a thousand, and two put ten thousand to flight? (Deut. 32:30).

Maybe 10,000 had come against us and we had only 1,000 trying to put the enemy to flight. That could explain our difficulty. I began to understand the need for a corporate anointing. Even though there were 200 intercessors praying, all lived in different places and prayed alone. What would happen if several intercessors in the same area came together for prayer? The scripture in Deuteronomy indicated that there would not be an addition or even a multiplication of prayer power—the scripture revealed *exponential increase* in prayer power when more than one person prays! I felt this was strategy from the Lord.

After more prayer for direction, I called Mary Cook. Mary was from my local church and has been known as an intercessor for several years. When explaining the need for a corporate prayer group, Mary responded by telling me how the Lord had been speaking to her about praying for me. How awesome is the Lord!

Within a few days, Mary had a group of powerful intercessors eagerly wanting to pray together for the ministry. Immediately after they started to meet together and pray, the attacks stopped. Since that time, the Lord has spoken to several other intercessors, and more corporate intercession groups have developed. What a strength and protection they have been to this ministry!

CORPORATE INTERCESSION

In 1995 in Singapore, while speaking to a conference for women pastors and leaders from throughout Southeast Asia, the Lord once again reminded me of the need for an additional prayer base. The ministry was now expanding into many nations of the world. After questioning the Lord about the new prayer base, I felt the need for intercessors in other nations to be involved. If I was to impact the nations, I needed international representatives as inter-cessors. During the conference about 20 people came to me saying the Lord had spoken to them to pray for my ministry. All this hap-pened without my telling them what I felt the Lord was speaking to me. The Lord was revealing strategy each step of the way.

Since that time, we continue to listen for the Lord's strategy in prayer in order to prevent backlash, or repercussions from the enemy. Individual and corporate intercessors in the United States as well as in several other nations continue to pray for us. Along with all this, we now close the office for a period of time each day. Those working in the office come together during this time for prayer and intercession. Since this is our base of ministry, we want to be sure the enemy has no access. Through all these times of change, the Lord has spoken strategy for prayer.

BACKLASH

The enemy does not stop his maneuvers to interfere with the will of God just because we have experienced a victory. He is stubborn in his pursuit to stop the plan of God. Therefore, he engages in an activity often referred to as backlash. One of Webster's definitions for "backlash" is "a quick, sharp recoil."[1]

Considering the fact that the enemy is likened to a serpent or snake, we can understand this definition. A serpent will recoil and try to strike a target he considers as his enemy. Satan does the same thing in spiritual warfare. Many times in spiritual battle, he will recoil and try to strike again after God's people have secured a victory.

David experienced a time when his enemies tried to come against him after a victory. In chapter 1 of this book we read about the Lord breaking through David's enemies like the breakthrough of waters (see 2 Sam. 5:20). A couple of verses later we find the Philistines trying to come against David again:

> Now the Philistines came up once again and spread themselves out in the valley of Rephaim (2 Sam. 5:22).

Seasoned intercessors are aware of these tactics and have learned ways to prevent many of these attacks. Although we have not yet learned how to guarantee the prevention of all attacks, we have learned ways to stop many of them.

PRINCIPLES FOR PREVENTING BACKLASH

As a result of seeking the Lord for strategy to prevent backlash from the enemy, several principles have emerged.

FAITHFUL FOLLOW-UP

The first principle for preventing backlash is to be faithful in follow-up prayer. Many times we engage in powerful times of intercession before a major event. Once the event is over and the victory is won, we let down in our prayer life. The necessity for intense prayer just doesn't seem necessary. However, that is usually the time we need to pray the most.

About a year ago I returned home after a trip to Malaysia. An apostolic team had accompanied me to minister at a national conference for a network of churches. During the time of ministry, the Lord had revealed much strategy for advancing the network and the churches. We were all aware of the supernatural wisdom of God during our time there. People were positioned in key places to move the churches ahead.

Within two weeks from the time of our departure, a couple of people died and several others were stricken with severe illnesses or had accidents. One of the key people ended up in intensive care at the best hospital in the country. For several weeks it looked as if he would die. The doctors ran every test possible. They ruled out every possible disease that could be causing the symptoms. There simply was no diagnosis and no hope for survival.

After learning of the problem, we alerted our entire network of intercessors to pray. The other members of the apostolic team did the same with their intercessors. Each morning, as soon as I was out of bed, I would check my e-mail to find out the condition of the young man, and then I would send out a daily report to the intercessors. While speaking at a church in California, we anointed a handkerchief with oil. Actually, we drowned it with oil! The elders, my husband and I prayed over the handkerchief, prophesied over it and released prophetic declarations. A tape recording of the prayer and declarations was sent along with the anointed cloth in an overnight package to Malaysia. They were then taken to the hospital room and the cloth placed on the body of the young man. Within a couple days, he was out of the hospital.

The enemy had recoiled for another attack, but intercessors continued to pray. We were praying a follow-up prayer. Victory had been obtained, but now we had to maintain the victory. Later I returned to Malaysia. The churches had reached a higher spiritual level and great progress had been made. Although the enemy tried to stop the plan of God, he was unsuccessful because the intercessors were faithful in follow-up prayer.

STEP-BY-STEP INQUIRY

Another principle in preventing backlash is to inquire of the Lord each step of the way. Although David had sought the Lord for victory in the past, he also inquired of the Lord with each new step he took. The strategy for one battle may not be the strategy for the next battle.

> And when David inquired of the LORD, He said, "You shall not go directly up; circle around behind them and come at them in front of the balsam trees. And it shall be, when you hear the sound of marching in the tops of the balsam trees, then you shall act promptly, for then the LORD will have gone out before you to strike the army of the Philistines." Then David did so, just as the LORD had commanded him, and struck down the Philistines from Geba as far as Gezer (2 Sam. 5:23-25).

I was reminded of this principle when the Lord spoke to me about the need for an increase in the base of intercession with each increase in the ministry. It was necessary to inquire of Him each step of the way to hear how to increase the prayer base.

GUARD YOUR HEART

A third principle in preventing backlash is to guard the heart. After a hard battle, it is easy to let anger, bitterness or even pride get in. Most cults have been started by people who at one time made at least a verbal profession of faith in the Lord Jesus. David Berg was such a man.

David was the pastor of a Christian Alliance Church. Over a period of time, there was strife between David and the congregation. After an inability to reconcile the differences, David left the church. He was hurt and bitter. Soon other hurt and bitter young people joined him, and they formed a group. Bitter spirits attract bitter spirits. The group wrote off society as doomed.

Deception entered and David saw himself as God's "prophet of the hour." A new church (cult) was formed, known as "The Children of God." Deception in David and his followers increased, and today "The Children of God" is one of the largest cults in the world.

The deception started with a root of bitterness that was never dealt with. Bitterness led to deception, which later led to immorality. We cannot afford to become bitter after a battle. The price is too high.

MAINTAIN CONNECTIONS

A fourth principle in preventing backlash is to maintain God's chosen connections in our lives. Several years ago a lady named Lana agreed to help with some assignments in the ministry. After a few months, I received a phone call from her.

"Barbara, I feel I need to resign from this position in the ministry. Everything has gone wrong since I agreed to help," she stated. "My finances have dried up. There is stress on my job, and now my father has had a heart attack. Maybe if I just stay home and not be involved, the enemy will leave me alone."

"That is exactly what he would like for you to do," I acknowledged. "If the enemy can get you to detach yourself from the
Body of Christ, he will not only eat your lunch, he will eat your
lunch bag also. The best thing you can do is get up out of your
chair and make the enemy sorry he ever showed up at your
door."

Lana saw the truth and volunteered once again to complete
her assignment. Jesus understood this principle when he sent
His disciples out two by two:

> And He summoned the twelve and began to send them
> out in pairs; and He was giving them authority over the
> unclean spirits (Mark 6:7).

When we are joined with other believers, there is an exponential increase in power. The church at Antioch sent Saul and
Barnabas out together as an apostolic team. The warfare they
would face would be intense. Neither would be able to ade-

INTERCESSORS ARE TOO OFTEN LACKING PROPER SPIRITUAL
PROTECTION, LEAVING THEM VULNERABLE TO SPIRITUAL
ATTACKS, DECEPTION AND THE FIERY DARTS OF THE ENEMY.

quately fulfill the task alone. Isolation leaves a person vulnerable
to further attacks from the enemy. The Bible calls the Church an
army. An army does not consist of a single soldier, but of many
soldiers joined together.

SPIRITUAL ACCOUNTABILITY

A final principle to prevent backlash is to be sure that you are
accountable to spiritual authority. Accountability is not a place

of bondage but a place of freedom. Too often I find intercessors without proper spiritual protection. These intercessors are vulnerable to spiritual attacks, deception and many fiery darts of the enemy.

I remember a situation in my life several years ago. I was speaking at a series of meetings in another state. One evening as I arrived, a man handed me an envelope.

"There is a word of encouragement inside," he said with a friendly smile.

"Thank you," I responded. "I can certainly use a word of encouragement."

I walked to the front of the room to begin the ministry for that evening. After the meeting, I arrived at my hotel room and reached for the envelope. I could hardly wait to read it. How thoughtful of that man to want to encourage me. Opening the envelope, I was shocked. What kind of "encouragement" was this?

"Barbara, if you don't repent, you are going to die and so will a large part of the Body of Christ," the letter read. I continued reading but the letter did not say what I was to repent of. It did not tell me what I was doing wrong.

Throughout the night I searched my heart to see if I could find a place of sin, a place of unforgiveness or a place of bitterness. The next morning I talked to the local pastor who was helping to sponsor the meetings. "Just forget the letter," he advised. "That man goes from church to church. He thinks he is a prophet and is supposed to bring correction to every church."

I appreciated the pastor's advice, but I wanted to be sure there was nothing in my heart or life that could bring harm to the Body of Christ. A couple of days later I phoned another pastor. I had ministered in his church several times a year for about five years. He knew my life in the pulpit and out of the pulpit. He also is a very strong prophet.

After reading the letter to him over the phone, Pastor Dwayne offered this advice: "Throw the letter away, Barbara. That is not a 'word'; it is a 'curse.'" I thanked him for the advice but still could not get peace.

When I returned home, I made an appointment with my own pastor. He read the letter and then counseled me, "Barbara, get rid of the letter. There is no truth in it."

Finally, I had peace. I had checked with several spiritual authorities in my life. I was accountable to them. As a result of our relationship, they had a right to speak into my life. All of them were in agreement. I then broke the power of the written "curse" over my life and the Body of Christ. Forgiveness was released to the man who wrote the letter. I then asked the Lord to put people in his life to bring correction and prevent him from bringing more pain and confusion to God's people. I could now continue doing what the Lord asked me to do without a feeling of guilt or condemnation.

How thankful I was for those people the Lord put around me. Accountability is a blessing from the Lord. The fiery dart of the enemy was stopped.

THE IRRESISTIBLE CHURCH

Jesus promised to build His Church and said that the enemy would not be able to resist this Church (see Matt. 16:18). As intercessors participate with the Lord in building His Church, we will be used powerfully in various types of prophetic intercession. We can engage in spiritual warfare without fear or intimidation. The Lord has given us principles to follow that will provide protection from the onslaughts of the enemy.

What a glorious day to be alive! What an awesome privilege to be counted worthy to participate with our Lord Jesus in subduing the enemy and releasing God's creation into its destiny through prophetic prayer!

QUESTIONS FOR CONSIDERATION:

1. Have you ever had a series of difficulties in your life in a relatively short period of time?
2. Did you seek and receive strategy from the Lord to solve the problems? What were you instructed to do?
3. When you are participating in spiritual warfare, do you enlist intercessors to pray for you? Why or why not?
4. Describe a time when you experienced backlash.
5. What are some of the various ways you inquire of the Lord?
6. How do you deal with anger or bitterness?
7. How will you now incorporate prophetic intercession into your prayer life?

ENDNOTES

CHAPTER 2

1. Dutch Sheets, *Intercessory Prayer* (Ventura, CA: Regal Books, 1996), pp. 82, 83.
2. Spiros Zodhiates, "Lexical Aids to the Old Testament," *Hebrew-Greek Key Study Bible, New American Standard* (Chattanooga: AMG Publishers, 1990), p. 1773.
3. Gary DeMar, *America's Christian History: The Untold Story* (Atlanta: American Vision, Inc., 1995), p. 7.
4. Sheets, *Intercessory Prayer*, p. 203.

CHAPTER 3

1. David B. Guralnik, editor, *Webster's New World Dictionary* (New York: World Publishing, 1972), p. 432.
2. Arthur R. Matthews, *Born for Battle* (New York: Banja Company, 1998), p. 54.
3. Jay Blevins, *Faith Must Be Developed* (Little Rock: Jay Blevins Evangelistic Association, 1977), p. 9.

CHAPTER 4

1. Jane Hamon, *Dreams and Visions* (Santa Rosa, FL: Christian International Ministries Network, 1997), pp. 104, 105.
2. C. Peter Wagner, *Lighting the World* (Ventura, CA: Regal Books, 1995), pp. 75, 76.
3. Herman Riffel, *Learning to Hear God's Voice* (Old Tappan, NJ: Chosen Books, 1986), pp. 49, 50.
4. Cindy Jacobs, *The Voice of God* (Ventura, CA: Regal Books, 1995), p. 145.

CHAPTER 5

1. Sheets, *Intercessory Prayer*, p. 27.
2. Guralnik, *Webster's New World Dictionary*, p. 173.
3. Sheets, *Intercessory Prayer*, p. 224.
4. Zodhiates, "Lexical Aids to the Old Testament," *Hebrew-Greek Key Study Bible, New American Standard*, p. 1780.
5. Ibid., pp. 1723, 1724.
6. James Strong, "Dictionary of the Words in the Hebrew Bible," *Hebrew-Greek Key Study Bible, New American Standard* (Chattanooga: AMG Publishers, 1990), p. 120.

CHAPTER 6

1. W. E. Vine, *Vine's Expository Dictionary of New Testament Words* (McLean, VA: Macdonald Publishing Company), p. 903.
2. Ibid., p. 607.
3. Zodhiates, "Lexical Aids to the Old Testament," *Hebrew-Greek Key Study Bible, New American Standard*, p. 1755.
4. Ibid., p. 1787.
5. James B. Jordan, *Through New Eyes* (Brentwood, TN: Wolgemuth & Hyatt Publishers, 1988), p. 139.

CHAPTER 7

1. Sheets, *Intercessory Prayer*, p. 83.
2. James Strong, *Strong's Exhaustive Concordance of the Bible, Greek Dictionary of the New Testament* (McLean, VA: Macdonald Publishing Company), p. 20.
3. Zodhiates, "Lexical Aids to the Old Testament," *Hebrew-Greek Key Study Bible, New American Standard*, p. 1772.
4. Ibid., p. 1845.
5. Ibid., p. 1848.
6. Guralnik, *Webster's New World Dictionary*, p. 1217.
7. Zodhiates, "Lexical Aids to the Old Testament," *Hebrew-Greek Key Study Bible, New American Standard*, p. 1820.
8. Ibid., p. 1852.

CHAPTER 8

1. Reported by Patty Redden and Earl Pickard, Wichita, Kansas. Used by permission.
2. Guralnik, *Webster's New World Dictionary*, p. 1139.
3. Ibid., p. 13.
4. Steve Hawthorne and Graham Kendrick, *Prayerwalking* (Orlando, FL: Creation House, 1993), pp. 97, 98.

CHAPTER 9

1. Zodhiates, "Lexical Aids to the Old Testament," *Hebrew-Greek Key Study Bible, New American Standard*, p. 1792.
2. LaMar Boschman, *The Rebirth of Music* (Little Rock: Manasseh Books, 1990), pp. 51, 52.
3. David Swan, *The Davidic Generation* (Kuala Lumpur, Malaysia: Tabernacle of David, 1993), pp. 33, 34.
4. C. Peter Wagner, *Blazing the Way* (Ventura, CA: Regal Books, 1995), p. 80.

CHAPTER 10

1. James M. Freeman, *Manners and Customs of the Bible* (Plainfield, NJ: Logos International), p. 67.
2. Sheets, *Intercessory Prayer*, p. 149.
3. Matthew Henry, *Logos Library System, Matthew Henry's Commentary on the Bible* (Peabody, MA: Hendrickson Publishers, 1997).
4. Zodhiates, "Lexical Aids to the Old Testament," *Hebrew-Greek Key Study Bible, New American Standard*, p. 1754.
5. Ibid., p. 1793.

CHAPTER 11

1. C. Peter Wagner, *Breaking Strongholds In Your City* (Ventura, CA: Regal Books, 1993), pp. 101, 102.
2. Hawthorne, Kendrick, *Prayerwalking*, p. 12.
3. "The Day the Idols Fell," *Charisma* (Lake Mary, FL: Strang Communications, January 1998), p. 40.
4. Sheets, *Intercessory Prayer*, p. 152.
5. Mike Haught. Used by permission.
6. *Pray Texas* newsletter, Volume 2, Number 4, August 6, 1998.

CHAPTER 12

1. Guralnik, *Webster's New World Dictionary*, p. 102.

To contact Barbara Wentroble or for more information about Wentroble Christian Ministries, please write or call:

WENTROBLE CHRISTIAN MINISTRIES

P.O. BOX 382107
DUNCANVILLE, TEXAS 75138
(972) 283-9199
FAX (972) 283-9198

E-mail: wcmin1@aol.com